MOST WANTED
IN
BRUNSWICK COUNTY

....

The Saga of the Desperado Jesse C. Walker

....

MARK W. KOENIG

THE
History
PRESS

Published by The History Press
Charleston, SC
www.historypress.com

First published 2023

Manufactured in the United States

ISBN 9781467154222

Library of Congress Control Number: 2022951586

Notice: The information in this book is true and complete to the best of our knowledge. It is offered without guarantee on the part of the author or The History Press. The author and The History Press disclaim all liability in connection with the use of this book.

CONTENTS

CONTENTS

PREFACE

The tale of Jesse C. Walker makes for interesting study. He first captured my attention when I was writing a book about a railroad in Brunswick County, North Carolina. One of the principals behind that railroad in its formative years was shot and killed in 1908 in sensational enough fashion to be reported in newspapers around the state. Following that thread of a story, I discovered that the victim's name spiked in mentions in 1909, 1915, 1919 and 1935. This was an unusual pattern for someone who was dead.

Digging through the newspaper stories, I found that the connecting thread was not the victim but the perpetrator. Details led first in one direction and then in another, playing out in episodes spanning thirty years or more. These stories became a body of knowledge that provided a foundation for a remarkable story that combined high-profile events, false names, prison escapes, thousands of miles of travel and more.

Research information was largely furnished by contemporary newspapers. Corroboration and fact-checking among them were inconsistent principles, and anecdotes or embellishments often substituted for verified information. As a result, the story found here is mostly based on what news articles reported, composed under the space constraints and often hasty timeline demands of daily publications. The assortment of weeklies had a bit more time but often lacked the depth of the dailies.

Our protagonist packed an awful lot of activity into a mere dozen years or so; the rest of the time, he apparently never rose to capture anyone's attention. Consequently, there are many missing pieces in what the reported narratives relate, and some conjecture is inevitable to fill in the gaps. I have attempted to fill these in with most likely or probable sequences, based on weighing alternative paths between known items and context. Such a course of reconciliation presents shortcomings, of course, but I have attempted to avoid fanciful supposition and accept that there may be mistaken interpretations.

One inconsistency among earlier news reports is that of Walker's name. Newspapers at times reported it as Jesse C., J.C., J.P., Jesse P., Jesse O. and other small variations. It seems that he most often used just his initials, J.C. Ultimately, however, most confidence can be placed with Jesse C., although the middle name was never spelled out. Perhaps in the haste of deadlines and typesetting, such errors regularly occurred, and proofreading was unevenly practiced. Some examples for other people included Robinson as Robertson, Wicks as Wick, Stanland as Standland or Stanaland and other minor variants.

There are also overlapping or inconsistent details among contemporaneous reports, as they were written with deadlines and press times looming. This was typical then as it is now; in today's frenzied news reports in the aftermath of sensational events ("Breaking News!"), they often contain differences that get ironed out over time. In Walker's story, these differences posed some small problems, even if they did not materially alter the basics of the story. In later years, news reports recapping Walker's exploits clarified things a bit, but some discrepancies remained. Walker himself tended to embroider his accounts in interviews or engage in some bits of dodgy logic, both unhelpful practices for the purposes of this work.

By good fortune, I was able to converse with J.R. Robinson, a descendant relative-by-marriage of the Leonard family mentioned in this work. His compilation of family histories and photographs was a valuable source of context for understanding the prominent families in Brunswick County. There are connections on top of connections among them, a dividend of large families, I suppose. Recollections of J.C. Walker are still preserved, albeit less brightly than they were several decades ago. There were more details about Jackson Stanland from Clinton Stanland, a great-grandson of the slain lawman.

Digressions cannot be avoided, since they serve to provide context to the events described here. I have tried to keep such items relevant as I incorporated them in the storyline. Walker's story is not a neat end-to-end linear narrative; details appear in later reports that were not disclosed earlier.

His activities touched on geography, terrain, settings, weaponry and cultural influences that sometimes need a bit more explanation.

There is a surprisingly large number of noted characters who appear in this chronicle of Walker's life; these include victims, accomplices, relatives, law officers, court officials, spouses and more. His affairs drew the attention of at least six governors in three states. At times, people disappear from the narrative, only to reappear years later. Who they are and where they touched the narrative are summarized in the appendices.

Where it seems warranted, there will be maps to help explain the areas under discussion. Since these maps were produced at different times, the scales and level of detail vary, and place names have a way of appearing and disappearing over the years. Nonetheless, they are helpful to illustrate movements of the main character.

Additionally, many newspapers simply printed telegraph dispatches from kindred publications. In going to typesetting, the articles' paragraphs could be reordered or edited to fit, leading to occasional typos or modifications. Regrettably, photographs were uncommon, and where they did appear, they were often unsuited to today's publication needs. Graininess or uneven inking were the usual culprits. Those images that didn't pass muster are described in the text.

At least until 1920, newspaper coverage was colorful in detailing Walker's exploits. Terms like *desperado, murderer, notorious outlaw, shiftless fellow, murderous-minded* and the like are sprinkled throughout news reports. One officer recalled Walker as "just about the roughest, toughest, meanest criminal a jail ever tried to hold"—surely a bit of hyperbole meant to capture attention. As always, headlines were designed to catch the reader's eye using lively words in a minimum amount of space.

At the end of it all, a body of knowledge has been assembled, matched as best as it can be for the events described at particular times and reconciled across time as later reports summarized previous episodes.

Let's get to it, shall we?

ACKNOWLEDGEMENTS

Grateful acknowledgement for support and assistance is given to:

Bob Surridge from the Southport Historical Society, a valuable source of information about Southport and its various institutions, names and places. Especially useful was a thorough tour of the Southport Jail, which was the setting for a pivotal episode in this story. His early reading of the manuscript provided details that might have otherwise been overlooked.

J.R. Robinson, whose extensive knowledge of the Leonard, Robinson, Holden and other families in Brunswick County provided enlightenment on the social and commercial relationships that existed over the years. Keepsake photographs helped bring to life some of the named persons in the story, and anecdotes provided glimpses of how the memories are preserved. He was able to "connect the dots" of several threads in the narrative.

Clinton Stanland, a great-grandson of Brunswick County Sheriff Jackson Stanland, whose encounter with Walker set off the central chain of events in the narrative. His recollections of family history were valuable in furnishing details about relationships and events during the period in question.

Mitch Henderson, whose good eye and hands brought to life to the grainy newspaper images of our main character.

The Brunswick County Historical Society, whose members dove deep into archived information to retrieve elusive but helpful bits of information about the county and its families, personalities and various enterprises. Some photographs were especially useful in illustrating what was going on in the area when several events in the narrative took place.

To my wife, Calverna, whose keen eyes picked out compositional goofs, whose patient forbearance allowed the spread of materials on various tables around the house and whose good-natured tolerance and encouragement permitted me to explore and develop the narrative of this work.

A DATE WITH DOOM

Early into the twentieth century, Brunswick County, in the southeast corner of North Carolina, was a quiet place. Covering about one thousand square miles, it had a population of only thirteen thousand or so and wealth, where it was noted at all, was more likely to be measured in acreage rather than dollars—one might be considered well off with an income of $1,000 a year. Two hundred years of subdivision had done little but carve the county into thousands of small parcels, where owners, for the most part, had to work hard to earn a living.

There were farm plots, to be sure, where a variety of garden and cash crops were grown—such things as rice, corn, peanuts, cotton, beans, sweet potatoes, seasonal fruit, tobacco and so forth. Along the coast, fishermen set out for catches of oysters, shrimp and fish, limiting their hauls to what could reasonably be expected to be iced and sold within a couple of days. Where livestock was kept, animals often roamed free around cleared land, hemmed in more often by dense forest and undergrowth along the margins than by fence lines.

By today's measure, towns were not much more than villages; almost any place with more than 100 people would be called a town. Even so, they were few and far between, and named post offices might have had 50 or fewer patrons. Southport was the county seat and largest of the group, where about 1,400 people lived within its confines, about 10 percent of the county's population. It lay along the Cape Fear River near the Atlantic Ocean and was about twenty-two miles downstream from Wilmington, the state's largest city at the time.

Something like this is what would have passed for a pretty good road in Brunswick County in the first few decades of Walker's life. More primitive versions would branch off from time to time, perhaps to logging camps or carved-out homesteads in the forested terrain. *Photograph by the author, 2022.*

Farther along the coast was Lockwood's Folly, never more than a cluster of dwellings around the mouth of the river of the same name. A few miles inland was the town of Shallotte, likewise along a namesake river as far as boats could go and where the colonial-era Georgetown Road crossed it. That road wound up through the county in a northeasterly direction, connecting the towns of Supply, Bolivia, Town Creek and El Paso before ending at a causeway leading to Wilmington. Off this main route was a network of primitive roads leading away to hamlets, settlements and farmsteads deep into the interior of the county or toward the Cape Fear River.

Except for a sprinkling of small cleared fields and farmhouses, Brunswick County was dominated by forest, mostly longleaf pine. In maturity, these trees stood well over one hundred feet tall and were prized for their durable straight-grained lumber. They also yielded sap, a mainstay for the economy of the region. This gooey liquid would be laboriously collected and distilled for turpentine, resin, pine tar and rosin—very important products for boatbuilding and general construction. The area's other tree species included oaks, cypress, cedar, sycamore, gum, hickory, dogwood and more, each valuable in their own way and sent to sawmills for processing.

About eight years into the twentieth century, the prospects for Brunswick County's economic future were beginning to brighten a bit. After twenty-five years of failed attempts and broken promises, a railroad was finally being built that would open up the mostly forested interior of the county. A few of the failed earlier efforts had managed to build fragments, but now, a company aimed to stitch them together for a route between Wilmington and Southport. A functioning railroad would be a big improvement for commercial and passenger traffic through the county, which was to this point dependent on unreliable roads and waterborne transport. At long last, there seemed to be the potential for capital to flow into the cash-strapped county and generate financial benefits.

In this domain, the top law officer was Sheriff Jackson Stanland. His forebears had been in the county for about one hundred years, and they were a respected presence among the area's old-line families of landowners, merchants, farmers and society leaders. He was a partner in a good mercantile

Around 1905, F.P. White and his wife, Sarah, pose outside of White's combination store and post office in Shallotte, North Carolina, handing mail to carrier Emery Stanley. The unpaved main street leads up a low hill, where several stores in the distance show that the town of only about 150 inhabitants was a commercial center in this rural part of Brunswick County. *Photograph from Leon Elwood Cheers,* Shallotte Centennial Commemorative Book *(Shallotte, NC: privately published, 1999).*

Jackson and Minnie
Stanland in a formal
photographic portrait,
likely taken around
1896, when they were
married. *Photograph
courtesy of Clinton Stanland,
family history.*

business in Shallotte, and farther out in the county, he owned more than
ten thousand acres of productive forest land, operated a gristmill and ran a
turpentine still in season. For good measure, he was also an investor in the
nascent railroad that was being built through the interior of the county.

With wealth and a good reputation, Stanland had the basic qualifications
to run for office. His first foray was a successful run for Brunswick County
treasurer in 1904; he was then approached to run for sheriff in the next
election cycle. Family memories recall that he was a reluctant candidate,
already having his hands full with business interests and a large family
crowded into a small house in Shallotte. Nevertheless, he was eventually
persuaded to accept the call and was elected sheriff for the first time in 1906.
As the Republican candidate in this solidly Democratic county, it was a bit of
a contest, but he prevailed. He was duly sworn in and settled into his office
in the courthouse in Southport.

Befitting his prominence, Stanland also was building a new house for
his family on an adjoining lot in Shallotte. There were seven children in
the household, and a more substantial house would be a welcome relief, he
thought, with more space for everyone and some modern conveniences. For
instance, Shallotte had telephone service, a handy means to keep in touch
with his affairs in Southport. He would have to see if he could get one of
those gadgets wired into his new house for himself. The county had almost
one hundred of these devices in service, and it would be a good time to get
on the exchange.

Now at age forty-six, Sheriff Stanland had just won another term in the
November 1908 election. Most of his activities were more or less routine.
He might be involved with the occasional seaman acting up while on shore,
breaking up moonshine operations (North Carolina was a dry state, but

Until 1908, Jackson Stanland was living in Shallotte in the house in the top image, certainly a crowded affair with seven children in the family. He was in the process of building the much larger house in the bottom image when he met his demise at the hands of Jesse Walker. *Photographs by the author, 2022.*

people will find a way), serving tax delinquency notices, overseeing auctions to settle debts, courthouse duties every three months and managing the jail with its prisoners, if any. Prisoners' confinements were usually brief, carried out while awaiting disposition when the superior court held its quarterly sessions. Penalties often consisted of working on the county roads, a never-ending endeavor, and the county got free labor in the deal.

All things considered, there were not very many crimes of note, and most of these were often minor in nature. Given the precarious nature of the area's roads and rare motor vehicles, speeding and traffic infractions were unheard of. There were only a few automobiles in the county—and only 1,600 in the entire state—and cars would only be registered starting in 1909. Property crimes were most often minor affairs, handled by township constables against known individuals within their tiny communities. Bodily crimes were likewise usually of a minor nature, perhaps an argument heating up into a brawl or maybe a domestic violence event.

It was the afternoon of November 29, 1908, when Sheriff Stanland was in his office at the Brunswick County Courthouse in Southport, North Carolina. He was probably unenthusiastic about spending time there on this chilly Sunday, but there was a troublesome errand nagging at him. In a couple more days, he would be sworn in for another term of two years, and he wanted to clear the errand off his desk before the month was out. He had some pending arrest warrants to serve, and with that done, he could approach his new term with a fresh slate.

For some weeks, he had been attempting to serve those warrants on a young man in the area, someone who had been under suspicion for breaking and entering at a store in the town of Shallotte. Further indications were that he had accomplices in the incident, including a teenage son of a prominent local family. The army also had a notice out that the suspect was wanted for desertion, which was outside of the sheriff's immediate authority but something he could assist with.

The sheriff had a bit of vested interest in the store-breaking event. For one thing, he had good businesses in Shallotte and farther down in the county, and he could imagine the insult felt by an owner when someone broke in. He likely knew the offended owner personally. For another thing, he was building his new house in Shallotte. There would be some value in his personal efforts to make sure that his home community was safe and secure. As he was going over some paperwork and gathering his thoughts, he might have planned to serve his warrants and head home for dinner.

But for him, dinner would never be served.

1

EARLY GOINGS

The subject of Sheriff Stanland's attention was one Jesse C. Walker. Much of what might be surmised about Walker's early years is, not surprisingly, fragmentary. Scant information has been gleaned in bits from later newspaper articles and public documents, occasionally with conflicting details. After one of his later exploits, Walker alluded to a biographical manuscript he was working on, but that alleged document had been lost during a chase. This was a time of limited communications, inconsistent record keeping and no centralized databases—the word *database* itself would be coined in the far distant future. It is a bit of a challenge to piece together the bits of what is available.

Walker was born in in the early 1880s—of that much, we are certain. Based on a marriage certificate and death certificate, a birth year of 1882 is noted. Newspapers gave various ages in their earlier reporting, yielding a birth year between 1881 and 1886. Later accounts become consistent enough to hint that 1883 was his birth year, although his grave marker is inscribed with the year 1882 (it also misspells his first name). Information from the 1900 U.S. census indicates 1884 as the year of his birth. As was very common for the time, Walker would have been born at home.

Like the birth year question, several possibilities arise as to the place of his birth. While Georgia, Florida and Oklahoma are mentioned in news reports, it is not until his 1946 obituary that a birthplace of Metter, Georgia, is mentioned—that town that will come into the narrative later. His death certificate also mentions Georgia as his place of birth, and this verifies information from the 1900 U.S. census. Confusingly, a marriage certificate and 1930 census record state Columbus County, North Carolina, as his place of birth.

~~~

Author's note: The shifting geographic focus of more than three hundred miles is somewhat difficult to reconcile. It might be that Walker's immediate family was on the move around the time he was born. Although not as common as today, families would relocate for various reasons, perhaps for better opportunities, to reconnect with kinfolk elsewhere or simply get away.

One possibility could be that he was born in Georgia, but the family moved soon thereafter to North Carolina. Walker could have remained in North Carolina with relatives as the rest of his family moved back to Georgia. As an infant, he could plausibly recollect that he was "basically" born in North Carolina, since that would have been his earliest memories.

Another possibility is that he was indeed born in North Carolina, but the family moved soon thereafter to Georgia—essentially a mirror image of the events described above. Perhaps at some point, the family returned to North Carolina while Walker was still a child but then moved back, leaving Walker with relatives. He recalled being with an uncle in North Carolina during a memorable event around Whiteville when he was just a lad. Later events also pointed to enduring relationships in Columbus County.

Some of this back-and-forth traveling may provide some justification why he went to Georgia in later years. He evidently had siblings there and then returned there after he was married the first time. There is some nexus in the storyline that is not fully understood, even though it doesn't significantly affect the overall arc of his story.

~~~

According to a marriage and death certificate, Walker was born to Robert T. Walker and Mary Baldwin Walker, both of North Carolina. Jesse's obituary also mentions younger brothers named Joe and Johnnie, who lived in Metter, Georgia, for some years before moving on to towns in Florida. From county marriage records, Jesse's father apparently remarried in 1898, perhaps after his first wife died. Two years later, the 1900 U.S. census lists nineteen-year-old Elizabeth (née Davidson) as the wife of Robert T., joining a household with three adolescent boys.

Later stories refer to Walker having kinfolk in the sparsely settled wild lands around Lake Waccamaw and Whiteville, North Carolina. Walker later

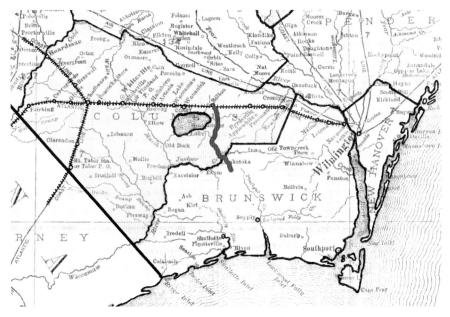

This map of Columbus and Brunswick Counties helps locate a tram line (highlighted) of the Waccamaw Lumber Company from the town of Bolton into the Green Swamp area. Walker grew up in this area and was likely familiar with the company's activity. New Business Atlas Map of North Carolina *(Chicago: Rand McNally and Company [detail], 1911); University of North Carolina at Chapel Hill Digital Collection.*

showed great familiarity with the area, and it may have been that he was sent there at a very young age and remained for a majority of his childhood. These relatives maintained very small and remote farmsteads, eking out their lives in what could be described as "off the grid" before there was even a grid to be off of.

Small-scale farming might have provided some seasonal income, and gardens and hunting provided food. Walker once alluded to being with an uncle on a trip to Whiteville. There were other occasional trips to the nearest town to obtain necessities that were unavailable at home, along with glimpses of the wider world beyond the rural confines of the farmsteads. Toward the end of the nineteenth century, the area surrounding the lake was heavily forested, as were the areas down toward the Green Swamp and further into Brunswick County. What "roads" were there were basically wide paths worn from use, and Walker's kinfolk lived on small clearings off these.

In his early years, Walker became very familiar with the forest byways, building a base of knowledge that would serve him well later on. Logging operations in the area had cleared a network of rough routes through the

Much of the Green Swamp was composed of savannas, or "islands" of pine trees with low ground vegetation, as shown in the upper image. The savannas were separated by boggy belts and depressions that were filled with scrubby brush and other trees. After clearing, grading, and channeling, much of the savanna land was converted to agricultural fields, as shown in the lower image. *Photographs by the author, 2022.*

native growth so that timber could be hauled out on a central tramway. Connections to the outside world were made on the Wilmington, Columbia and Augusta Railroad, running on nearby tracks westward out of Wilmington through Delco, Bolton, Lake Waccamaw, Whiteville and points beyond. A few more or less durable roads led to these towns, and one threaded through the Green Swamp area to the southeast and Southport.

Walker's education in the 1890s would have been solid but basic, typical of the period in the rural South. He got as far as the fifth grade (according to the 1940 U.S. Census) and was literate, could write and do his numbers. He apparently was also personable and able to engage sociably with others; he was a perceptive and quick learner and adept at mechanical contrivances. These traits would come into play in years to come.

While the young Walker and his relatives in the backcountry may have struggled in the 1890s, they were not alone. In the larger economy, a money crisis and five-year double-dip depression drove bank failures, financial hardships and unemployment throughout the country. The effects may have been a bit muted in North Carolina, depending as it did on agricultural commodities instead of manufacturing and finance. But at least two railroad projects in next door Brunswick County failed during these years, and with them went hopes for economic benefits in the southeastern part of the state.

2

ON THE MOVE

Walker was too young to directly appreciate the effects of the hard times (one could not get much lower than subsistence living), but they may have affected his outlook. Trips to town and exposure to the effects on businesses there would provide at least a superficial awareness of economic conditions. It may be that he also conceived a desire to strike out for better prospects when he was able. In a later recounting (*Charlotte News and Observer*, July 17, 1936) he apparently had a bit of an epiphany while walking through the woods with an uncle. He claimed that he was awed by the light streaming through the trees, but he was too young to take it as anything more than a memorable experience.

The young Walker may have latched on to a couple of dime novels on trips to town or from local friends. These cheap, widely distributed and very popular publications usually catered to young male readers and featured romanticized adventure tales. Here one would find formulaic stories about the wild frontier, detective mysteries and even life as a hobo. To an impressionable lad stuck in the wild backlands of North Carolina, these tales may have stimulated a desire to launch his own adventures. There were places to go and adventures to be had, and excitement awaited.

It is also possible that Walker may have crossed paths with real-life hobos traveling on freight trains through the area. Beyond Whiteville was Chadbourn, a junction town with rails going north and south, east and west. The mid-1890s were dealing with a major depression and high unemployment, and many men took to the rails to seek any form of gainful

A "road" before decent paving was developed or even necessary. It was wide enough for a team and wagon; such lanes were crowded in by brushy verges and woods. Lacking anything so refined as surveys and planning, these roads wandered off in all directions in the undeveloped areas of Brunswick County. They might have served as extended driveways to farmsteads or connections to small settlements. *Photograph by the author, 2022.*

occupation. The South, with its agriculture-based economy, needed seasonal workers in the fields or extra hands for forest cutting, and an itinerant workforce provided a solution.

While hobos were nearly always just "passing through," they might stay in a place for a while to earn some cash before moving on. They also brought with them tales of far-away places, adventures, humor and advice—all of which could be absorbed by an impressionable youth with an itch for something more than a backwoods life. In Nels Anderson's seminal work, *The Hobo: The Sociology of the Homeless Man*, the effect of this tale-telling is summarized quite neatly.

> *To boys the tramp is not a problem, but a human being, and an interesting one at that. He has no cares nor burdens to hold him down. All he is concerned with is to live and seek adventure, and in this he personifies the heroes in the stories the boys have read. Tramp life is an invitation to a*

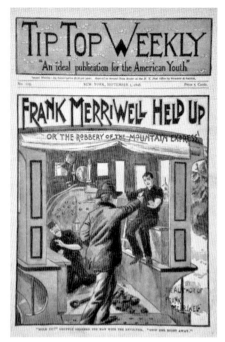

Dime novels of the late nineteenth and early twentieth centuries provided young male readers with exciting tales of derring-do in the Wild West and other exotic locations. One popular series even recounted lively tales of a hobo's life, usually skipping over the hazards and dangers such a lifestyle encompassed. *Pinterest.*

career of varied experiences and adventures. All this is a promise and a challenge. A promise that all the wishes that disturb him shall be fulfilled and a challenge to leave the work-a-day world that he is bound to.

In a few years Walker found the opportunity to strike out on his own; a later record notes that he left home at age fifteen, about 1898 or so. If his home at the time was in Metter, Georgia, this would have been shortly after his father remarried. His stepmother was only three years older than Walker, and it is not hard to imagine some tensions as she was integrated into an established family. After some wandering, he eventually found his way down to Claxton, Georgia, some twenty miles distant and fifty miles west of Savannah.

According to a later report (*Raleigh News & Observer*, February 21, 1909), it was recollected that Walker found employment in Claxton selling parlor organs, pricey but desirable houschold furnishings of the time. He probably signed on as a route salesman with a dealer in a larger town and called on prospects to promote the cultural and aesthetic virtues of these instruments.

Case 370

Made in solid oak and walnut finish.
Size: Height, 82 in.   Width, 47 in.   Depth, 23 in.
Oval top French beveled mirror, 12 x 18 in.
Made in five and six octaves.

Walker reportedly had a brief stint trying to sell parlor organs on instalment plans in Georgia. While these were considered a sign of culture in a household, they could easily have cost more than a month's hard-earned wages to purchase. *Pinterest*.

While he had some success collecting down payments, he apparently pocketed some of the proceeds that he collected and was being sought to answer for the missing funds.

A quick departure found him back up north in Metter. He may have sought refuge with his family, but even that may have been a little too close to Claxton for comfort. Both towns were in Bulloch County, and the sheriff there may have distributed notices. At this point, he could have made his way farther north to Augusta, where several rail lines converged and where he would find a train back to familiar territory and among kinfolk in North Carolina near Lake Waccamaw and Whiteville.

When he got back, the Waccamaw Lumber Company was busy in the area, having secured ownership and timber rights to as much as two hundred thousand acres of forested land in Columbus and Brunswick Counties. Along with clearing out trees, the company also cleared access roads through to reach stands of marketable timber. For a while, the company even considered laying in a railroad to Southport, perhaps by extending a tramway already threading through the area. These roads provided new routes through what had been essentially trackless territory and a figurative invitation to anyone willing to explore where they went.

Walker took up that invitation and made his way down to the town of Shallotte in lower Brunswick County. In a later news report, he presented himself as a "picture agent" when he arrived in the area. This would be an itinerant occupation, presumably working for a photography company. Perhaps he fancied himself one of those characters who were looking for models to supply to artists engaged in the booming growth of illustrated magazines. This might be a trade somewhat akin to later Hollywood "talent scouts" enticing young women with movie ambitions. He might even have managed to latch on to a camera and photographic apparatus.

A logging train being loaded up in the Green Swamp area, which was being cleared by the Waccamaw Lumber Company in the early 1900s. Note the clear-cutting approach in the pine savanna. Cleared tracts were to be repurposed for field crops and truck produce. *Photo courtesy of Brunswick County Historical Society.*

With his friendly manner and knack for spinning narratives, his purported occupation would easily justify the roaming lifestyle in his backstory. To be sure, the trade had its fair share of scam artists and hustlers, and if a quick getaway could be had, such characters could be on the move after collecting fees from gullible prospects. This was an age where credentials could not be easily verified, and his apparent sincerity may have alleviated doubts when he met people. Some may have even thought of him as an ambitious up-and-comer, full of youthful optimism. Ultimately, though, the story was just a fiction.

Walker made the acquaintance of Frank M. Leonard. His family had been in Brunswick County for over one hundred years with predecessor branches of the family dating to colonial times. Leonard ran an implement and hard goods store in Shallotte, trading in farming equipment and tools, tack and harness, wagon parts, iron goods, hardware, cordage and the like. He also owned and farmed land around Shallotte and about ten miles away near Lockwood's Folly. His properties abutted those of other longstanding families, with a good deal of intermarriage among them.

Leonard had been in town and around Shallotte all his life—in short, he was a well-established and well-known presence in the area. He had married well and benefitted from his association with reputable citizens and old-line society. When Walker arrived, his presence would also become well known; with only a couple hundred inhabitants in and around town, new people would have been noteworthy. Curiosity about Walker would fuel any number of conversations as he attached himself to the established Leonard family.

It is not too difficult to imagine that Walker ditched his "picture agent" pretense relatively soon. It would be unsustainable around a town where cash was hard enough to come by for necessities, much less for such fripperies as potential modeling gigs. It might be that he hired out for a more reliable position working in Leonard's store or even as a farmhand on the family's holdings. His work may have been in exchange for lodging and meals and a bit of spare cash—not an uncommon arrangement for the time and area. He also got to know the family, the elder Leonard and

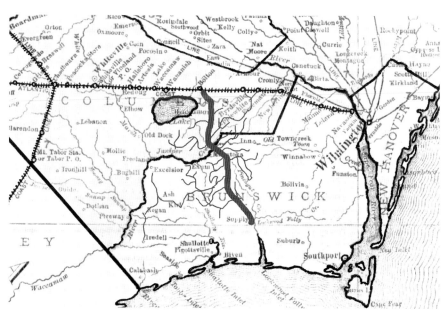

A map of Columbus and Brunswick Counties helps locate just one road of any significance (highlighted) between the oval-shaped Lake Waccamaw, through the Green Swamp area and down to Supply. Here, Walker could pick up the road to Shallotte, where he drifted down and met his first wife. New Business Atlas Map of North Carolina *(Chicago: Rand McNally and Company [detail], 1911); University of North Carolina at Chapel Hill Digital Collection.*

Jesse Walker and Rosa Lee (Leonard) in a youthful pose. This image was probably taken around the time they were married in 1905. Walker was a cherubic twenty-two years old, and Rosa Lee was seventeen years old. *Photograph courtesy of J.R. Robinson, Robinson family history.*

his wife, along with their five children ranging in age from about three to sixteen years of age. He could have spun out tales of his travels and adventures, maybe with a bit of exaggeration. Naturally, he would suppress details about his legal problems.

One impressionable child was young Frank A. Leonard, who was about ten years old. With two older sisters and a brother, Frank may have latched on to Walker as a more exciting older companion. Here was someone who brought enticing hints of lively times beyond the lad's world of rural existence. Walker was about ten years older, and this relationship would come into play in later episodes, as we will see. His credibility was not universally accepted, however; according to Robinson family histories, the grandmother in the household was deeply skeptical of Walker's glib charms and resolutely distrusted him.

He seemed to make another kind of impression on young Rosa Lee Leonard, about seventeen years old. According to family recollections, she was a bit of a "live wire" herself and may have been taken by Walker's tales of his experiences. This relationship took a romantic turn, and they were married on August 6, 1905, by a justice of the peace in a small wedding at a friend's house well out of town in Lockwood's Folly. Living in a small town and working for his father-in-law were probably not satisfactory arrangements, however, and before long he set out to change them.

With his wife, Walker moved back to Metter, Georgia. Whatever motivations he may have had are unclear, although there were some tensions within the Leonard clan. Perhaps he sought to reconnect in an

In August 1905, Walker married Rosa Lee Leonard, a daughter of the family with whom Walker had taken up near Shallotte, North Carolina, sometime after his foray into Georgia. The couple would return to Georgia, and in 1907, their daughter Clara Lee was born. *Register of Deeds, Brunswick County, North Carolina.*

area familiar to him and some miles and years removed from his infractions in nearby Claxton. He still had family there, and they might have taken the young couple in. One newspaper account mentions that he believed he was still owed payments from his illicit organ-selling scheme. He may have tried to collect on those—not a terribly wise objective, considering.

His time in Metter was brief, however. A later anecdote in the *Wilmington Dispatch* (March 8, 1915) recounts how Walker was angered by an incident while he was there.

> *Somebody killed a kitten belonging to Walker…and this so enraged him that he got on a drunk, went to the church next day and raised a disturbance with those accused of killing the cat. The result was that he left Metter immediately, returning to his wife's home in Brunswick* [County]. *His wife was ill at the time and she did not come until later.*

Before long, then, Walker was back in North Carolina and back among the Leonard family. If this was any time during the latter part of 1906, his wife, alluded to above, was carrying their child, something which would not have been said "out loud" in the newspaper. A daughter, Clara Lee, was born in Georgia in February 1907. Shortly thereafter, mother and daughter moved back to the family home near Shallotte. It must have been a difficult situation. Walker had no livelihood, was probably an unwelcome presence in a family of standing, had a trail of infractions and now had an infant daughter.

At this point, several reports have Walker as having enlisted in the army and reporting for training. This might have been a convenient way to escape detection by authorities; he still had active charges of embezzlement against him, along with whatever complaints may have arisen from his outburst in Metter, Georgia. A passing note in one newspaper article mentions desertion from Fortress Monroe in Virginia, which would be extremely unlikely. Other reports suggest desertion from a post in Georgia, perhaps confused with his recent Georgia residency. Another account mentions desertion from Fort Caswell near Southport, just twenty miles away. The last may be most likely, given the short time frames involved during this period. In any event, he quickly determined that army life was not for him and deserted.

Walker could hardly have been considered a model citizen when he got back to the Shallotte area, having added desertion from the army to his list of liabilities. Over the course of the next year or so he gained a reputation as a "roving, shiftless fellow" according to news accounts. Among so few residents of the area, his presence would have been known and commented on. Undoubtedly, he became a blot on the good name of the Leonard family, but he retained the friendship of his young brother-in-law Frank Leonard. His wife would have largely seen to the care of their daughter and likely endured a degree of disapproval from their circle of friends and acquaintances.

Disapproval would soon be the least of the problems.

A PECK OF TROUBLE

FELL DOING HIS DUTY

SHERIFF STANLAND MURDERED.

Brunswick Officer Shot Down by Desperate Man in County. White Man, Suspected of Fired into Posse sults Sunday Night

Sheriff Jackson Star ck county, was sh Sunday nigh

THE BRUNSWICK TRAGEDY.

Mr. J. J. Knox May Succeed Late Sheriff Stanland—Other Arrests.

Mr. J. W. Brooks returned yesterday from Shallotte, Brunswick county, where he attended the funeral of the late Sheriff Jackson Stanland, whose tragic death occurred last Monday night after being shot the night before by the white man Walker. Mr. Brooks says the services were attended by a great gathering of the friends of the popular sheriff, whose loss as a citizen and as an officer is greatly deplored.

The young man Dudley, arrested the day after the tragedy on suspicion of being an accomplice in the st robbery for which Walker was arr ed at the time of the killing of Sh Stanland, is believed to be a bro of the principal in the killing. arrested he is said to have had a belt of skeleton keys strapped a his person and the circums against him are very strong. F jail at Southport. Young Fran ard, Jr., a brother-in-law of and a mere lad, who was als ed in the same connection, w ed after being arrested upon $50.
It is said to be practica

SHERIFF MURDERED

Brunswick Officer Shot Down by Desperate Man in Lower Part of County.

DIED WITHIN 24 HOURS

White Man Named Walker, Suspected of Storebreaking, Fired into Posse With Fatal Results Sunday Night—In Jail.

Sheriff Jackson Stanland, of Brunswick county, was shot and fatally

Sheriff Stanland, of Brunswick County, Fatally Wounded While Arresting a Storebreaker.

Sheriff Jackson Stanland, of Brunswick county, was shot and fatally wounded Sunday night by a white man named Walker, upon whom he and a posse of three others were serving a warrant for storebreaking, at Walker's home near Shallotte, in a remote part of the county. Sheriff Stanland died Monday night. Walker and two other white men named Dudley and Leonard, who were arrested later as confederates, were placed in jail at

Walker's path was about to intersect with that of Sheriff Jackson Stanland, whom we met earlier. Ordinarily, Stanland found that his duties were straightforward and undramatic. It would be with some interest, therefore, that he began to hear things about Jesse Walker. Here was a young fellow who had appeared in the area several years earlier with a bit of a sketchy background. Relatively quickly, he had married into a well-known and long-established family, left shortly after with his wife and returned without her. Then there was talk

The *Lumberton Robesonian*, *Wilmington Morning Star* and *Smithfield Herald*.

about him having enlisted in the army and deserting. Walker would be someone to keep an eye on, for sure.

The sheriff may have not been aware of Walker having had an occupation; if he had any recollection of him being a "picture agent," that pretense had long evaporated, and he was not engaged in regular work. Walker's activities may have centered on petty theft and minor grifting. He drifted around the area, perhaps with a few odd jobs or day labor gigs to earn a little money and assess places for "supplemental" rewards. In today's parlance, he might be said to have lacked "marketable life skills." Somewhere along the line, he also managed to obtain a ring of skeleton keys, along with a temptation to become proficient in their use. This set the stage for his next chain of events.

Walker was apparently devising some new plans, although they were not very carefully thought out. He was about to go beyond the boundary of small-scale scalawaggery into territory he considered more lucrative. In the fall of 1908, he somehow persuaded young Frank Leonard, his brother-in-law, to help him check out some of the stores in Shallotte. They could note when the stores were open, when the owners retired, if they locked their doors at night, if dogs were present and so on. Another young lad, William Dudley—hailing from Georgia, so it was said—drifted into the area and joined the pair, and a couple of break-ins occurred.

Of course, Sheriff Stanland heard of these; after all, he was building a house in Shallotte and would be aware of the store breaking incidents in town. Suspicion fell on Walker as the "odd man out" around the area, and the sheriff had also received some notice from the army about his desertion. By the end of October, the sheriff had arrest papers drawn up and figured on serving them. Walker caught wind of what was going on and made himself scarce, while the sheriff let it be known that he was being sought.

Walker was known to be in the area; after all, his wife and child were living at his in-laws, and he felt some allegiance to stay nearby. However, he had proven to be a slippery rascal, and the sheriff had been unable to serve him warrants for the store breaking incidents in Shallotte and his desertion from the army. If Walker had been advised by family members or acquaintances to take the initiative and turn himself in, he ignored their advice. Now, at the end of November 1908, the time had come to finally make the delivery and resolve this situation.

Sheriff Stanland received word on November 29 that Walker was at his father-in-law's house near Shallotte. Relying on this tip and with his

Brunswick County sheriff Jackson Stanland, shown here around 1896, when he was thirty-five years old. His fatal encounter with Jesse C. Walker in 1908 set off a series of episodes that made headlines over the next twenty-five years. *Photograph courtesy of Clinton Stanland, family history.*

familiarity of the area, the sheriff decided to act promptly and serve papers on this character. As he considered his next steps, he might have thought that the errand was enough out of the ordinary that some extra help would come in handy. He called together three other officers to form a posse. Together, they set out for Shallotte to hopefully pen in the suspect before he could slip through their grasp again.

Riding out to the house in a couple of buggies, they quietly approached the house in the darkening evening. Nearer, they could hear some loud arguments going on inside. Given Walker's talent for evasion, the sheriff refined his plan to increase his chances of success. After peeking through the window to see that his target was present, the sheriff instructed two of his posse to go to around the back of the house. The aim was to have them enter at the same time he entered from the front. A deputy and another officer split off to take the rear entrance, and the sheriff posted the remaining officer in the front yard. When all was ready, Sheriff Stanland knocked on the door, entered and announced that he was serving his warrants. And that's when things went terribly sideways, setting off a chain of events that would make headlines for the next twenty-five years.

Walker, now cornered and confronted, quickly produced a pistol from where he had been holding it in his lap. It was a new model Colt army-issue semi-automatic pistol, and he reflexively pulled back the slide to cock it and opened fire. How he obtained the weapon, issued to army officers, was never explained; perhaps it was a "souvenir" from his brief stint as an enlistee. He may have been unfamiliar with the operation of the weapon, as he emptied the magazine in a spray of bullets, even as his arms were being restrained by one of the deputies.

Several bullets struck Sheriff Stanland, causing severe and mortal internal injuries. In the struggle, Deputy J.E. Robinson was also injured, as a bullet grazed his arm (we'll hear more about him later). The other officers quickly subdued Walker, even as his last rounds were being fired. The injured sheriff was able to stumble out of the house to the yard, where

The weapon taken from Walker when he shot Sheriff Jackson Stanland in 1908 was similar to this army-issue Colt .45-caliber semi-automatic pistol. This was a new design to meet the army's requirements, and it carried a seven-round magazine. Walker may have been unfamiliar with its operation; when apprehended, he emptied the magazine in a spray of bullets, at least three of which hit the sheriff. *GunsInternational.com.*

he collapsed. Despite his wounds, he remained conscious and was able to reason through the next steps. He instructed his officers to restrain Walker and take into custody his suspected accomplices, the young Frank Leonard and William Dudley. As soon as possible, they were to take the trio to Southport to be held for further developments.

Sheriff Stanland was carefully removed to a nearby home. He was likely aware of his prospects and recommended a successor to be designated by the county commissioners. From Shallotte, Dr. J.A. McNeil rushed to the scene of the shooting to render immediate aid, and a call was put out to Dr. Arthur Dosher in Southport. That doctor quickly arranged for a motorboat to take him down to the scene, a trip of about thirty miles more reliably made by water than over the roads in the darkness. Another call was made to Little River, South Carolina, just fifteen miles away, where another physician promptly headed toward the scene.

Walker was bound and taken to a store in Shallotte for an overnight stay. Once there, updates and instructions were relayed across the telephone wires up to Southport. A photograph taken the following day shows Walker in front of the store with his hands and upper arms tied; the officers apparently were not expecting to need handcuffs for what should have been a routine chore. In the image, Walker appears clean-shaven with a neutral expression. He was described by authorities as standing at five feet, six inches tall and weighing about 160 pounds; he had wide shoulders, blue eyes and a fair complexion.

Presented with the severe nature of the sheriff's injuries, there was little the physicians could do. Their examination indicated significant internal bleeding and damage, and they could only offer comfort until he died the next day. His body was put on a boat to Southport, and in a couple of days, a well-attended funeral was held there to commemorate his passing.

Left: Walker in 1908, after being held overnight in Shallotte. His hands and upper arms were bound in preparation for transport to the Brunswick County Jail in Southport. *Drawing from a newspaper photograph by Mitchell Henderson, His Lead Studio; author's collection, 2022.*

Right: The memorial monument for Jackson Stanland (1862–1908), who was buried in the family plot of a cemetery in Shallotte, North Carolina. *Photograph by the author, 2022.*

The sheriff was laid to rest a few days later at a cemetery just outside of Shallotte in a family plot, with an imposing marble monument to mark his grave.

His tour of duty was over. His name would be inscribed on the North Carolina Peace Officers Memorial when that was erected in 1995.

4

GO TO JAIL, GO DIRECTLY TO JAIL

Walker was taken to the Southport Jail as quickly as possible, both for his own protection and to be held for further action. The sheriff was a popular figure in the area, and the deputies were aware of the potential for "rough justice" from his friends and associates. Lynchings were not unheard of during these years, but such impromptu expressions of local outrage created all kinds of investigative headaches. Walker's accomplices Leonard and Dudley (both about fifteen years old) were also jailed. The young Leonard, coming from a reputable and long-established family in the county, made bail and was released into the custody of his family.

It was deemed that preparations for arraignment and trial for the three could not be made in time for the next session of superior court. The court was due to be convened in just a couple of days, and notices had already been issued and the docket set. Walker and Dudley were ordered to be held until the next session of the court in March 1909. They were registered, escorted to their cells and fitted with ankle shackles, which were secured to a chain and ringbolt set into the floor of their cell. Whatever they were wearing served as their prison clothes; the county did not begin issuing distinctive uniforms until many years later.

The pair now resigned themselves to a stay in the recently built county jail. Unlike previous versions of the prison that had been damaged by storms or fire, this building was designed specifically to updated standards. When it was bult in 1904, it featured a fireproof and storm-resistant construction and

The Southport Jail as it appears today, operated as a museum by the Southport Historical Society. Built in 1904, it was fitted with the latest of confinement and security measures. The jailer's quarters shared the first floor with intake and duty rooms, while the second floor was divided into spaces for different classes of security and holding. *Photograph by the author, 2022.*

was fitted with modern fixtures of confinement. It had structural exterior walls of brick that were sixteen inches thick and interior brick walls that were twelve inches thick. The second floor and roof were constructed of cement poured over metal corrugated "barrel" forms.

Perhaps reflected in its low cost of $6,738 (the modern-day equivalent of only about $250,000) the building lacked such refinements as central heat or air conditioning, electricity and plumbing, and water was hand pumped from the backyard. At the time, this was true of most of Southport's buildings. These features would have to wait several more years, or even decades, to be installed. Half of the first floor contained living quarters for a jailer and family, although space was quite limited. A separate entrance was designed for their convenience and to segregate these quarters from the activities of the jail proper. Other than inside the jailer's quarters, all doorways were fitted with a solid iron door and a strap-iron grille door, both keyed.

Walker and Dudley were led upstairs to the confinement areas. Rather than being placed in low-security holding cells, they were brought into the high-security portion of the jail. What awaited them were two cells measuring about eight feet square, set away from the barred windows. They were walled with strap-iron grille, and there was a sheet metal ceiling and dividing wall between them. Sliding doors on the cells were manually released from the outside, and when they were opened, prisoners could exit through a narrow and grilled passage along the front to a locked door. The entire construction was surrounded on three sides by a wider walk-around passage, and the room itself had a secure keyed double door. All in all, it was basically a cage within a cage within a cage.

Walker now had over three months of waiting to endure before his case could be brought to trial—perhaps less than that if a special court session could be called (it wasn't). His world had shrunk down to an eight-by-eight-foot cell, while Dudley was held in the neighboring cell. The two of them could converse quietly, and from time to time, either of them might be allowed to pace a bit more along the grilled lane fronting the pair of cells. On occasion, one or the other might even be let out to take a bit more exercise on the walk-around lane outside the cells—under guard, of course. Here, Walker could look out of the barred windows, take in some fresh air if they were open and get better knowledge of his surroundings.

Walker had always been an easy conversationalist; having a bit of celebrity status, he may have attracted a few curious passersby on the ground below. Engaging them if the windows were open, he could find out more about his surroundings and pick up bits of news about what was going on. In casual comments, he could also get some idea of where he was in Southport— it was his first visit—where the boundaries and roads were and the like. There might have also been visits from whatever attorney had been chosen to represent him for his upcoming court appearances, although there is no mention of legal counsel in reports.

There are no indications of Walker being a difficult prisoner; apparently, without a weapon in his hand, he behaved well and presented no problems. At least for the first couple of weeks, he established a pattern of compliance and docility, perhaps engaging the guards in friendly banter and sending his compliments to the jailer's wife for the meals she prepared. The watchful diligence of these early days may have relaxed a bit as he adjusted to the routine of confinement. Exercising a degree of disarming cordiality, he may have even received some special meals from the kitchen as the Christmas holiday approached. If a later item is to believed, Walker may have also been

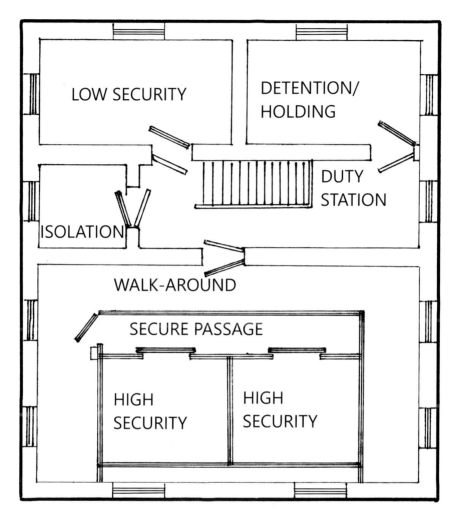

In this approximation of the second-floor plan of the Southport Jail, the arrangement of confinement quarters is shown. Walker and an accomplice were held separately in the high-security cells after the shooting of Sheriff Jackson Stanland late in 1908. After two months, they effected an escape, overpowering the jailer and leading pursuers on a chase into the wild areas of the Green Swamp. Walker slipped past the manhunting posses, but his fifteen-year-old accomplice very willingly surrendered. *Drawing by the author, 2022.*

working on a biographical manuscript describing his exploits, perhaps under the pretext of assisting his defense when the time came for trial.

After years of roving, however, the hours stretched out, and Walker began assessing his next moves. He would have noted that the stout construction of the jail presented some formidable deterrence, but it was also virtually soundproof, particularly when the doors to the room were closed. Out of idleness, but perhaps displaying some innate ingenuity, Walker began using his long periods of unattended cell time to loosen and break off a portion of the iron straps that served as a support for the straw mattress of his cot.

Christmas came and went, New Year's Day came and went and Walker was a crafty, busy man in January 1910. By all appearances, he was still compliant, affable and well-behaved, and his strict confinement may have eased up a bit. Perhaps he could be trusted for periods outside of his cell, albeit still in the cell room and under guard. During the lengthy times between eyes-on supervision, however, he apparently began fashioning a means of escape. He may have also felt a bit of regret at having dragged young Dudley into this predicament. It could be that in quiet conversation, he promised to get the lad out, so he encouraged him to be ready for action.

With the piece of iron from his cot, Walker diligently scraped and abraded the restraint chain fastened to the floor of his cell. Taking great care, he managed to weaken but not break it, deceiving the guards who routinely

Folded up is one of the 1904 cots in a high-security cell at the Southport Jail. Walker apparently broke off one of the strap-iron mattress supports and used it to plan and execute his 1909 escape. *Photograph by the author, 2022.*

secured him in his cell. He also patiently shaped a crude but potentially passable false key, likely calling on his experience in break-ins. It may be recalled that he had a supply of skeleton keys with him at the time of the fatal incident with the sheriff. The cement floor would have proved a serviceable grinding surface; long periods of back-and-forth abrading would gradually achieve a desired dimension.

During periods outside of his cell, Walker could have surreptitiously tried the fit of his makeshift key in the door keyways, gradually approaching a point where it could be inserted. Careful observation of the keys the guards used, perhaps dangling from a belt, would yield clues about the shape of the key blade. The locks themselves were sturdy but had basic catchment mechanisms, familiar in their action to a man of Walker's experience.

Walker had a motive, and he had the means—now, for the opportunity.

5

THE END OF A BRIEF SOJOURN

riday, January 29, 1909, was a routine day for J.B. Fountain. He was the deputy sheriff in charge of the Southport Jail, a part-time position that, under ordinary circumstances, was not very demanding. That suited him just fine; he had operated a grocery and foodstuffs store since the 1890s and was a well-liked merchant in Southport's small business district. Besides shelf goods, he provided baked products, candies and confections, tobacco, occasionally meat and, perhaps most popularly, an ice cream counter. He also owned a livery and feed stable and had recently bought into a steamboat company. He was a man of many interests, by all accounts.

Other deputies provided coverage when he was not at the jail. Jesse Walker and Will Dudley were his special prisoners, and they were confined to their cells. They had been locked up after the late Sheriff Stanland's murder and were awaiting trial, scheduled for early March. In another secure room, a suspected arsonist spun out his time waiting for his court date. On this chilly afternoon, Fountain may have strolled over to the business district, perhaps to fetch some supplies from the store or to catch up on whatever was newsworthy around town. There might have been some messages waiting for him at the telegraph and telephone building, and the post office and sheriff's office at the courthouse were also on his route.

Meanwhile, Sheriff John J. Knox, who had succeeded the late Jackson Stanland, was absent from the office. He was out in the county with his brother, delivering tax notices and making collections. He was postmaster in

The Brunswick County Courthouse is where quarter sessions of the superior court were held to hear and decide cases. The building, erected in the 1850s, also held the sheriff's offices and records department. At the time of Walker's 1915 apprehension, the building was plain brick; the portico and stucco were added in later years. *Photograph by the author, 2022.*

the on-again-off-again tiny community of El Paso and had been elected as a county commissioner in 1908. At the request of Sheriff Stanland, he was appointed to fill the dying sheriff's term. His current errands would have been a routine part of his activities. With the day getting dark, though, it was time to head back to Southport. He had acquired one of the first of those newfangled motorcars in the county, and he was probably enjoying the ride with his brother along the newly improved Southport-Supply Road—a full ten feet wide. With business done for the week, he could wrap things up and enjoy a quiet couple of days. His weekend was about to be trashed.

After returning to the jail, Jailer Fountain may have worked a bit on end-of-week reports or started a duty roster for the next week. His wife would be preparing meals for them and the prisoners or thinking about what to prepare for the weekend, maybe a bit of pick-up-and-put-away choring. As it grew dark, Fountain received an end-of-shift report from his duty guard— all three prisoners were quiet and behaved as usual, check-up rounds all in

A revolver similar to this Iver Johnson .38-caliber was taken from Southport jailer J.B. Fountain when Walker broke out for the first time in 1909. Fountain was a small man, so this petite five-shooter would have been a handy weapon, somewhat smaller than some handguns but with enough firepower to deter attackers in close quarters. It was fitted with an internal automatic safety feature so that it was impossible to fire accidentally. *icollector.com.*

order, keys transferred, logbook updated and the like. He relieved the guard and went to his quarters to check on the prisoners' meals.

Once the meal trays were prepared, he took them up the stairs to the prisoners, delivering one to the suspected arsonist who was being held in a low-security cell and the other two to Walker and the lad Dudley. Opening the solid outer door of the cell room, Fountain checked to make sure that the two prisoners were in place. Then he unlocked and opened the inner grille door and brought in the meal trays, locking the inner door behind him. The prisoners were in their cells with the sliding doors latched and in place, so everything there seemed to be in order. It was pretty dark in the room, so Fountain lit the lamp to at least provide some modest light. He may have thought that it would be nice if the county commissioners rigged a power line to the building so there would be electric lighting—people seemed to be impressed with it.

Fountain unlocked the door to the narrow passage outside the cells and placed a tray down outside of each. He may have exchanged some pleasantries with Walker, who always seemed to be sociable. Dudley, on the other hand, was probably in a gloomy mood; being jailed at the age of fifteen in connection with a murder was not much of a spirit booster. Then he retreated to the passage door, closed it and secured it with a chain, probably intending to lock the door itself later when he retrieved the meal trays. At this point, he unlatched and retracted the cell doors so Walker and Dudley could get their meals and checked the room over once more. Then he exited through the double cell room doors, locking them behind him.

Now that the prisoners had been tended to, Jailer Fountain probably went downstairs to take his own meal and chat with his wife for a while. Upstairs in the cell room, Walker broke apart the chain he had patiently weakened, freeing his legs. With the narrow exterior passage open, he wolfed down his meal and proceeded to attack the chain holding the passage door shut, eventually breaking it with the iron strap he had broken off his cot. The jailer went back upstairs after his meal and assumed his post at a duty desk near the front of the building, maybe with some reading material to pass the time and little reckoning of what was about to happen.

Sometime around seven o'clock, he heard a noise from back in the corridor that led to the cells. After getting up and strolling down the corridor, he unlocked and opened the solid outer door to the cell room. A quick glance through the grilled inner door seemed to assure him that things were normal in the dimly lit room; it was time to pick up the meal trays, anyway. Upon opening the inner door, he was struck immediately by Walker, who was waiting outside of his line of sight to the side. The fragment of strap iron Walker had in his hand now became a weapon, and Fountain was beaten down and stunned. He was slight of build and easily overpowered by the more muscular Walker.

Walker relieved the jailer of his weapon, an Iver Johnson .38-caliber revolver, a few cartridges, keys and nippers, a tool to cut through chain or shackle fastenings. Quickly now, he freed his young accomplice Dudley, who was unenthusiastic about launching into any more adventures with the older man. Walker also opened the cell of the suspected arsonist, who wisely decided to stay put, and the pair fled down the stairs and out the door into the night. Jailer Fountain recovered enough to raise a commotion, which alerted his wife, and she aroused the neighbors. Two months to the day after he had been taken into custody, Jesse Walker was on the loose.

Sheriff J.J. Knox, who was appointed to fill the remainder of the term of the late Jackson Stanland. He organized the search efforts and dispatched posses throughout the county, following Walker's escape from Southport in 1909. *Photograph courtesy of Brunswick County Sheriff's Office.*

Sheriff Knox was just pulling into Southport when his son ran up and told him of the escape from the jail and injuries to the jailer. He drove into town and over to the jail, where he promptly summoned help from among the townsfolk. He posted some teams to roads leading out of town, hoping to keep Walker and Dudley within its modest confines. With Walker's lead time, however, it was not likely that the escapees were anywhere nearby. For good measure, telephone calls were made and telegrams sent to various destinations in those networks.

The sheriff quickly organized and dispatched posses and sent them to watch at greater distances from the town. With lanterns and torches, they rapidly set out northward to monitor the upper and lower bridges across Town Creek, some fifteen miles away. The shoreline along the Cape Fear River in Southport was also guarded in case the pair of fugitives should try a water escape. An attempt to get a team of bloodhounds from Wilmington was unsuccessful, so a telegram was sent to Burgaw, about forty-five miles and some hours away. Within a short while, however, it was learned that another tracking team was immediately available at Chadbourn in Columbus County and could arrive on the train in Wilmington that evening, where they would directly take the steamer down to Southport on a chartered run.

The chase was on.

6

THEY SEEK HIM HERE, THEY SEEK HIM THERE

WALKER OVERTAKEN

Brunswick Fugitive and His Accomplice Routed by Sheriff's Posse; Latter Taken.

NEAR BOLTON LAST NIGHT

Dudley Arrested But Murderer Into Swamp Before Fusilade Shots—Prisoner Brought Here on Way to Southport.

After an unremitting chase s... last Sunday n... time with the ... bourn, through ... of miles of ar... and posse, of ... night a few n... overtook J. C. ... iff Stanland, ... storebreaking, ... whom broke ... Friday night, ... ped on his kn...

REWARD.

For the arrest and delivery to me I will pay a reward of $100 for Jap P. Walker and for the arrest and delivery of one Dudley...ed as an accomplice with W... ...urder of Sheriff Jackso...

MAY BE HEADED THIS WAY

Brunswick Fugitives Closely Pursued Are Believed to be Making For Railroad—Rewards Now Nearly $1,000.

CLOSE TRACK OF WALKER

Fugitive Desperado From Southport Jail Seen Near Lockwood's Folly and Sheriff and Posse Gone in Pursuit.

A telephone message to Mr. J. W. Brooks, of this city, from County Commissioner Asa Dosher, of Brunswick, states that a report has reached Southport from an authentic source that J. P. Walker and his accomplice, Dudley, charged with the killing of Sheriff Stanland last November and who broke jail at Southport Friday night after a murderous assault upon the jailer, had been seen on Mr. Richmond Gollway's place, three miles from Lockwood's Folly bridge, in a remote part of the county, yesterday morning and that it is believed that it is only...

A PROCLAMATION BY THE GOVERNOR.
$250 REWARD.

State of North Carolina, Executive Department

...ereas official information has received at this department has Walker, late of the county of vick, stands charged with the of Jackson Stanland, and ...er has fled the State, or so himself, that the ordinary ...f law cannot be served upon

...erefore, I, W. W. Kitchin, ... the State of North Caro... ...rtue of authority in me ...ue this my pro... reward of Two Dollars for the ...ery of the said ...eriff of Bruns... ...urt House is ...oin all officers ...d citizens to criminal to

WALKER NOT TAKEN

Murderer of Sheriff Jackson Stanland Who Broke Southport Jail Still at Large.

EFFORTS TO RECAPTURE HIM

Two Bloodhounds From Burgaw Joined in Unsuccessful Chase Yesterday—Further Reward to be Offered—The Jailer.

In spite of unremitting efforts on the part of Sheriff J. J. Knox, his deputies and the people of Southport and Brunswick county at large, with all the assistance that could be rendered

he pair of escapees, now free of the jail, quickly surveyed their surroundings and probably made for the cover of piney woods just a block away that defined the edge of Southport. There were no streetlights to illuminate their way; the town would only get its first one later in the year. However, a nearly full moon shed enough light to avoid the headwaters of Bonnet Creek so they could skirt their way around to a road.

They were not about to try to find a local hiding place; they could probably already hear the alarm being raised. Under Walker's lead, they struck out to put as much distance as possible between them and those in pursuit. They likely made pretty good time using roads that were almost certainly empty on this cold winter night. One such route may have been the straight-line Southport-Supply Road, where more primitive roads branched off toward Shallotte and the area where Walker's wife and child were living with family.

That area was also laced with creeks and streams, presenting a series of navigational challenges and geographic cul-de-sacs. With Walker's knowledge of the area, it would not take him long to realize that such areas could be cut off and he would be trapped. There were a couple of makeshift ferries across the waterways, but using them meant unacceptable exposure. Overnight and into the next day, the pair may have tried a few alternate routes to get to more familiar surroundings where Walker might be able to cajole someone into giving them aid.

With options running out, however, Walker and young Dudley backtracked and struck out to the north, where there was better hope of intercepting roads that would take them up toward Walker's kinfolk around Lake Waccamaw. Along the way, there might be some aid in their trek. In the event of any encounters along the narrow tracks, they could beat a hasty retreat to the brushy margins crowding the edges of the roads.

The next day, Sheriff Knox posted a reward of $100 for Walker and $25 for Dudley. A special bill had been hastily introduced in the state legislature authorizing the county to post another $400 reward for Walker—dead or alive—and it was marked up for action and signed by Governor W.W. Kitchin. Another $60 had been raised from private sources, and the state itself chipped in another $250 to declare its sense of outrage. Considering this occurred on a weekend, these actions were remarkably speedy.

The reward was now up to $860, or over $25,000 today, a handsome incentive indeed for a cash-poor area. The entire southern half of the county was certainly on the alert, and the news was quickly spreading farther afield. A team of tracking hounds and a handler were secured from Burgaw after all, and they took the train to Wilmington. At that point, they made their way to the river and boarded the morning steamer to Southport, where they joined the first team in trying to strike a trail. A "wanted" poster was printed and distributed that carried a photograph of Walker and details of the reward.

REWARD!

$850.00 For the apprehension and delivery of J. P. Walker to the Sheriff of Brunswick County, at the Court House at Southport, N. C.

J. P. WALKER,

J. P. Walker is wanted for the murder of Sheriff Jackson Stanland, of Brunswick County, near Shallotte, N. C., in November, 1908. He subsequently broke jail and has since not been heard from. For his arrest and delivery as stated above, a reward of $850.00 will be paid; $400 by the County of Brunswick; $250 by the State of North Carolina, $100 by myself as Sheriff of the County, and $100 by a former business partner of the late Sheriff.

Description :---Walker is about 5 feet 6 inches tall, weighs about 160 pounds, wide shoulders, short neck, fair complexion, blue eyes, wide cheeks, large jaws and sharp chin; dark auburn hair, inclined to be a little curly when long, wears about No. 8 shoe.

All officers and all good citizens are asked to assist in bringing this criminal to justice. Write or telegraph,

J. J. KNOX,
Sheriff of Brunswick County.

El Paso, N. C., Feb. 10, 1909.
Pease Post.

The poster advertising a reward for the capture of Jesse Walker issued by Brunswick County Sheriff J.J. Knox in 1909 after Walker's escape from the Southport Jail. It lays out particulars of the crime and reward money, along with a description of Walker. Given the area's scarce telephone coverage, respondents were asked to write or telegraph the sheriff. *Photograph courtesy of Tom Vernon, from an article in* North Carolina Peace Officer *magazine (Summer 1997).*

These activities were avidly reported in the newspapers; this would have been big news after the sensational murder of the Sheriff Stanland just a couple of months earlier. Not surprisingly, tips and suggestions came in from all over, both accelerating and confusing an organized effort. Southport residents reported sightings in town, and more were reported from around Lockwood's Folly and near Shallotte, where Walker had his wife and child. However, hints of greater credibility were soon received from up toward the Green Swamp.

Wilmington businessman J.W. Brooks, a friend of the late Sheriff Stanland's business partner, coordinated efforts to keep the lines of communication open among authorities. Wilmington had ample telephone and telegraph service, along with connections with several railroads. Messages could be received and relayed quickly among various interested parties. Wilmington also had the only newspapers published in the area, and updates could be provided to them and sent out in telegraphic dispatches throughout the state.

Like today, various pundits and experts weighed in with gratuitous comments opining on various topics: criticism about the design of the jail, the quality of the chains, Walker's presumed promise to not be taken alive, Walker burning down the forest before he would be captured, the directions he would be likely to go, his villainous character and so forth. If there had been television, one can imagine the furrowed brows and frowny demeanors of such commentators. The *Charlotte Chronicle* evidently ran an out-of-date picture of a former jail building in its issue, prompting the following defense from the *Wilmington Morning Star* (February 2, 1909):

> *The* Charlotte Chronicle *does Brunswick County an injustice in publishing an old cut of the jail of that county as the present county prison. Its picture is of the old jail, which was pulled down some years ago and supplanted with a modern building. Brunswick has a first-class, up-to-date county prison now. Few counties in this state have better, and it is still a mystery how the prisoners made their escape from their cell last Friday night.*

In just a couple of days, search efforts began narrowing toward the area between Lake Waccamaw and the Green Swamp. These areas were very familiar to Walker, and logging operations had cleared large portions of them, with a tram line and access trails laced throughout. By February 2, reports had been received from logging camps that the two fugitives had been spotted in the area, asking for food. Almost immediately, however, they dashed back into the rougher areas, sensing that their pursuers were not far away. Searchers noted broken ice in some ponds, surmising that the two had cut across to throw off the trailing hounds.

A watch had been in effect lower in the county, below Shallotte. There were early reports of Walker in that area, where his wife and daughter were living with her family. Based on incoming reports, however, that watch was relaxed, as attention shifted to the Green Swamp area, about twenty-five miles away. And just a bit beyond that, the railroad out of Wilmington offered more possibilities for escape.

A fresh team of bloodhounds was brought in, and the sheriff deployed them to try to strike the trail of the fugitives. Several logging camps from the Waccamaw Lumber Company were also operating in the vicinity, and logging crews were asked to assist the posses and report suspicious activity. About seventy-five men were now involved in the effort as they gradually constricted the search area. An advisory was sent to the railroad to be vigilant, paying extra attention to the nearest stations and rural way stops.

Temporary tracks laid directly on native grade provided a means for extracting harvested timber from the Green Swamp. In this photograph, a loaded train is making its way through the cutting area to a sawmill. If Walker was aiming for the tracks in his escape, they would have provided a far more reliable way to traverse the area than cutting cross-country or following meandering roads. *Photograph courtesy of Brunswick County Historical Society.*

Up in the Green Swamp, Walker and Dudley trudged on. Here, they would have found those savannas, where pine trees spread a canopy over low vegetation, now pretty well reduced in the middle of winter. Unfortunately for the fugitives, these areas were also being cleared by the Waccamaw Lumber Company, and being spotted was a clear possibility. More than once they had to plunge into mucky and boggy spots and scrubby, overgrown streams that defined and separated the savanna areas.

The manhunt was beginning to close in on Walker and Dudley. The searchers had been hard at it for five days in the middle of winter. There were places where snow was on the ground, and if they were fortunate, there might be footprints as well. In the interlacing boggy areas, ice had formed on standing pools of water, and broken areas might also yield clues for the searchers—although the Green Swamp was inhabited by a variety of wildlife that would also break the ice to get a drink.

Besides coping with cold temperatures, the posses needed to be fed and accommodated, the dogs needed tending, and senses needed to be alert to signs of the fugitives. There might have been scant comfort in knowing that their quarry had it worse, but they persistently drew the search to tighter confines. If earlier sightings were credible, the pair of fugitives, in four days, had trailed nearly sixty miles in a circuitous path through the wilder parts of the county.

The posses' persistence paid off on February 4, when Walker and Dudley were at last confronted in Columbus County between the town of Bolton, which lay along the railroad tracks, and Livingston Creek a few miles to the east. As related in the *Wilmington Morning Star* (February 5, 1909), a half-accomplished goal was reported.

> *A little after 7 o'clock last night in the road near a branch, Mr. William E. Maultsby and Mr. Applewhite, both of Town Creek, and members of the posse, saw two men and advanced upon them. Mr. Maultsby called out to them to halt, and Dudley immediately dropped to his knees and surrendered. Walker, without showing fight, ran into the swamp as Mr. Maultsby opened up on him with a Winchester and Mr. Applewhite with a shot gun....The firing attracted other members of the posse very soon, and men were thrown out in all directions to surround the swamp, which is known as "Jesse Island," a part of the Green Swamp territory.*

Young William Dudley was held at the scene as the posse awaited the approach of a Wilmington-bound train. The train was flagged down, and

Work camps operated by the Waccamaw Lumber Company in the early 1900s, where dormitories and a dining hall accommodated the crews. Walker and his accomplice attempted to find some sustenance in at least one of these camps following their escape from the Southport Jail in 1909. *Photograph courtesy of Brunswick County Historical Society.*

the fugitive was escorted into Wilmington. He would be held there until the next morning, when he would be boarded on the steamer for a return trip downriver to Southport. Walker, under the cover of darkness and with his familiarity of the terrain, found temporary concealment in the wilder growth and then raced to find an exit before the posse could spread out and surround him.

It was reported that Dudley was relieved at being taken into custody; he probably saw it more as a rescue than a capture. He was near exhaustion and very cold, with his clothes wet and torn from the flight through the backcountry. Now free of whatever persuasive influence Walker had, he was glad to be able to talk about the experience. Having only recently arrived in the Shallotte area and joining up with Walker, he had intended to somehow find a way to go out west. Unfortunately for him, he had been persuaded to get some traveling cash from Walker's plans for pilferage.

He surrendered some keys, perhaps those taken from the Southport jailer when they made their escape. At Walker's instructions, Dudley was supposed to keep the keys for some unnamed friend of Walker's. He said that when he was freed from the jail, he was forced to accompany Walker, even though he would have been willing to quit the attempt from the outset. He related how the two of them had managed to stay just ahead of pursuit in those cold days and nights, darting across open areas and slogging through the many creeks and rough spots in the terrain.

At times, Dudley said they were within earshot of the tracking teams and even within range of their firearms, had they been spotted. To throw the dogs off their scent, they had apparently rubbed kerosene and sassafras root on their shoes—materials likely swiped from one of the several logging camps in the area. Dudley even related how Walker was bragging about not being taken alive and hopefully taking someone with him. He was still armed and considered dangerous with the Southport jailer's little pistol, although he had only four cartridges.

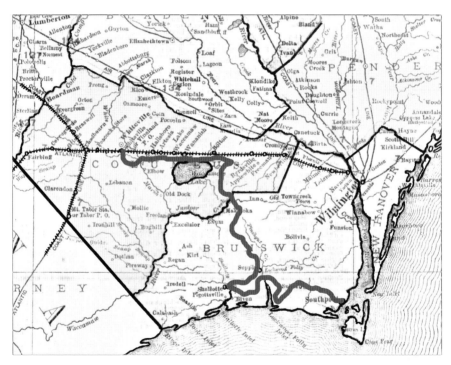

A map of Walker's circuitous movements (highlighted) in southeastern North Carolina following his 1910 escape from the Southport Jail. Some of the reports are difficult to verify given the distances and timeframes; Walker's movements would have been made entirely on foot and often over rough terrain. New Business Atlas Map of North Carolina *(Chicago: Rand McNally and Company [detail], 1911); University of North Carolina at Chapel Hill Digital Collection.*

And where was Jesse Walker? The search area was now well-defined, and the posse, along with volunteers from the Waccamaw Lumber Company, set to work early the next day (February 5) to comb through trees and brush. After a day and a half, however, it was clear that Walker had slipped through their hands and was gone. The situation was reported in the *Wilmington Morning Star* (February 7, 1909), and the story was not optimistic:

> *While hopes of ultimately effecting Walker's capture are not entirely given up, it was considered that after his escape from the swamp in which it was thought he had been effectively bottled up Thursday night, there was no use to undergo further privation and hardship with the chances so much against immediate success.*

Walker evaded the dragnet and apparently sped to the margin of Lake Waccamaw, where he was allegedly spotted. The prevailing opinion was that he had made his way there to hook a ride on one of the freight trains that was rolling through the northern part of the area and was some distance away by now. It may have been cold in the middle of winter, but things were way too hot for Walker, and he made a last dash to get out of the area. It was time to put a lot of distance between him the scene of his exploits.

The sheriff and other authorities extended thanks to everyone, the posses were decommissioned, the logging crews went back to work, the dogs and teams were sent back and trust was given to the reward money to motivate people in other jurisdictions to keep their eyes open. In its recounting, the *Wilmington Morning Star* closed its story with a grudging acknowledgement of Walker's resourcefulness and stamina, despite the nature of his crime and violent escape.

Some reports said that Walker had been seen along one or another of the various railroads that headed away from Wilmington, but they also pointed out that one tramp at a distance looked much like any other tramp. An anecdote from Bolton, nearest the northern boundary of the Green Swamp area, related that a man there had been held up. A newspaper was also taken from him, which the robber read with interest, as it described the intense search going on. Another report said a man told officers that some rough stranger had robbed him of his lunch pail. Later reports had Walker near Lumberton (in the next county to the west), Burgaw (in the next county to the north), Georgia (in his old haunts around Claxton and Metter) and even Florida. All proved to be false sightings.

The Atlantic Coast Line Railroad had a line that extended west out of Wilmington and went toward Whiteville and the junction town of Chadbourn. One of the stops along the way was Lake Waccamaw, often a day trip destination for recreation. It is presumed that Walker managed to hop on one of the trains that was passing through to make his escape in 1909. *Photograph courtesy of Wilmington Railroad Museum.*

In March, young William Dudley was convicted on several charges related to the store breaking incidents in Shallotte and the escape. Given his youth, peaceful surrender and domination by Walker, however, he was not given an extreme sentence. After his trial in Brunswick County, he was sentenced to about twenty months on a chain gang, working on the roads in Columbus County. What became of him is unknown.

Are we ready for a change of scenery?

7

GO WEST, YOUNG MAN

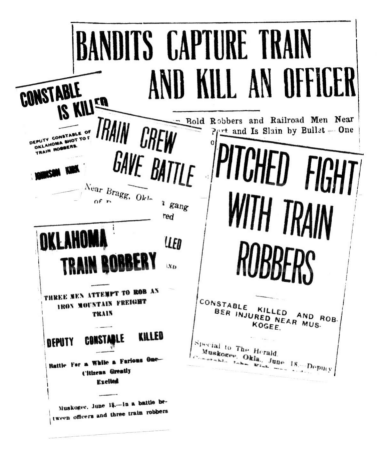

On a warm June morning in 1909, things were quiet in Braggs, Oklahoma. The village was never more than a whistle stop on a branch of the railroad, lying along the edge of Arkansas River bottom farmland to the west and a range of forested hills to the east. The closest town of significance was Muskogee, about fifteen miles away, just

The *Enid Daily Eagle, Ardmore Daily Ardmorite, Supulpa Light, Guthrie Oklahoma State Capital* and *Shawnee Daily Herald.*

inside the Creek Nation. Unknown to everyone, a Western drama was about to be played out, with those towns having central roles.

Some details were reported in quick dispatches at the time, while others followed shortly after or even a few years later. The reports described variations in how the events unfolded, reflecting hasty and overlapping accounts, but they all led to the same climactic conclusion. In the aftermath, one of the perpetrators was pretty talkative; his view of events is summarized in a later section.

Brewer Township constable Wick and his young deputy George Johnson Kirk had stopped at Braggs to exchange pleasantries. Deputy Kirk was only twenty-three years old, was well-liked in the area and had a wife and child. A photograph on the website Officer Down Memorial Page (*www. odmp.org*) shows an earnest young man looking somewhat uncomfortable in his suit. The deputy and constable were making the rounds, catching up on news and happenings, perhaps commenting on growing crops in the fields toward the river.

As recounted in a later and more reflective account, a St. Louis, Iron Mountain and Southern freight train on its way north slowed down through Braggs. This was the first section of a two-part shipment, and the crew passed a message along noting that three rough characters, likely hobos (or tramps, or "desperate-looking characters"), had tried to take passage on the train. They had been discovered and thrown off the train after a confrontation a couple of miles back. The second-section train would be along shortly—perhaps the crew on it could give an update.

The officers promptly mounted up and headed south along the tracks toward Illinois (now Gore, Oklahoma), about ten miles away from Braggs, and the second section of the freight train. It had stopped at the Illinois depot, where the four-man crew (engineer, fireman, brakeman and conductor) received their pay envelopes. As was customary, their wages were paid in cash—paychecks would come sometime in the future. After a bit of conversation, the engineer gave his signal, and the train eased forward on its northward haul.

About two miles short of reaching Braggs, the engineer on the train spotted an obstruction on the tracks and slowed down. Close up, it could be seen that someone had stacked some crossties on the tracks, and the train came to a halt. The crew was instantly on alert at this unexpected development, and three desperate-looking men dashed out from nearby bushes. Two of them approached the cab and threatened the engineer and fireman with revolvers, while the third climbed into the cab to steal the trainmen's pay envelopes.

In Oklahoma, the St. Louis and Iron Mountain Railway ran some of its trains on the tracks of other railroads. One of these trains was involved in the botched holdup attempt made by Paul Williams (Jesse Walker) and two accomplices. *Photograph courtesy of the Missouri Pacific Historical Society.*

The venture would present considerable risk for little reward. Split three ways, their expected takeaway would not have amounted to much, perhaps just enough to tide them over until they reached some undefined next destination. In the words of Nels Anderson, in *The Hobo: The Sociology of the Homeless Man*, "Hobos are not clever enough to be first-class crooks nor daring enough to be classed as criminals." This might suggest the degree of desperation they had to even make the attempt.

At the back end of the train, the conductor and brakeman were prepared for such unpleasant surprises, this part of the country still holding some aspects of the fabled Wild West. They grabbed their handguns and jumped off the caboose, approached the front end of the train and opened fire on the would-be bandits. The situation now became a shoot-out as the robbers retreated from the locomotive and sought cover at the crosstie barricade.

Constable Wick and Deputy Kirk heard the gunfire and galloped to the scene, where they reinforced the efforts of the crew. The robbers were now caught between gunfire from the train and gunfire from the constables approaching from the opposite direction. In the exchange, Deputy Kirk was shot in the head and instantly killed. The fatal shot was determined to have come from the man who had been in the cab of the locomotive.

Two of the robbers took advantage of a lull in the shooting to flee and headed off on the run up into the forested hills. The remaining man, suffering gunshot wounds to the chest, eventually fell and was restrained by the defenders. He was relieved of his weapon, a Colt .45 pistol. After clearing the barricade, they loaded the dead deputy and the wounded robber onto the train and pulled into Braggs. Once there, the wounded robber identified himself as Paul Williams and received basic medical attention from a young local physician. Deputy Kirk was a well-known and popular figure in the area with a wife and young child. Arrangements were quickly made to transport the wounded prisoner to Muskogee. Despite the circumstances of the incident, Constable Wick was in no mood to have to face down a lynch mob.

In short order, messages were telegraphed to the surrounding towns, and newspapers picked up on the story. Indeed, within a day, the story was printed in at least ten states, spreading from Texas to the Dakotas and eastward as far as New York and South Carolina. More far-flung reports tended to be short filler articles, but the incident apparently caught the eyes of editors looking for news from the western frontiers.

The trio were probably ignorant of the fact that train robberies, however notorious in fiction or on the silver screen, were becoming uncommon, having peaked in the 1890s. Railroad security, faster trains and better communication through telegraph and telephone systems all helped reduce the frequency of these crimes. Then, too, newspapers had moved away from covering such incidents as sensational, daring events and possibly inspiring more of them. Instead, they covered them as serious property crimes in which the perpetrators deserved whatever punishments would come to them. Despite being part of romanticized Wild West folklore, train robberies were increasingly prosecuted as truly menacing, and they used a wider array of tools available to law enforcement.

In Oklahoma, a posse was quickly formed from local farmers, and they set out to seek the two remaining fugitives. Aided by bloodhounds and a Cherokee tracker, the posse followed the two men who had apparently sped to the northeast toward Tahlequah. Just a short distance into the chase, a satchel containing lock-picking and breaking-and-entering tools was recovered. The team worked their way on horseback until they encountered dense forest. A deputy sheriff and the Cherokee tracker determined they would continue on foot and sent their horses back with the rest of the posse.

Eventually, the pair of pursuers encountered a work crew on a railroad line through the hills. From them, they borrowed a handcar to follow the line into Proctor, over thirty miles away from the scene of the crime. They learned that the fugitives had been spotted there but that they had not stayed long. Later that day, they were apprehended where they were camping outside of town. Exhausted and unarmed, they surrendered willingly but were quick to deny doing any of the shooting and laid the blame solely on the man already in custody. The two were arraigned in short order and entered pleas of not guilty, but Williams was too wounded to appear in court and would be arraigned later.

Paul Williams (Jesse Walker) used a weapon similar to the one pictured when he and two accomplices attempted a train robbery in Oklahoma in 1909. The legendary Colt .45-caliber six-shooter was two and a half pounds of deadly steel. It was widely carried throughout the West and became a staple in popular tales and films. *SportsmanOutdoorsSuperstore.com.*

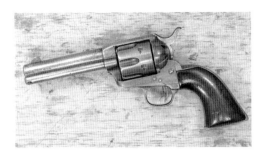

~~~

A summary of one of the accomplices' comments appeared in the Muskogee Times Democrat *on June 28, 1909. After further condensation, the newspaper article and his version of events are as follows:*

Fred Donaldson was one of the pair of fugitives who were apprehended around Proctor, Oklahoma, after an exhausting chase of over forty miles through hills, forest, streams, and otherwise rough country. Once they were cornered, they willingly gave up, probably glad to be taken into custody. The pair entered pleas of not guilty at arraignment, but Donaldson took the trouble to craft a written statement of some length in which he laid out his version of events. His version appeals to sympathy and clearly attempts to claim a lenient sentence.

He described how he had run away from home in Florida at the age of sixteen and had eventually signed on for sea shipping, with stops in South America and as far as Australia. After tiring of that, he wandered around the South, eventually picking up work here and there. Some months earlier, he had crossed paths with Williams, and the two became itinerant sign painters and wound up in Oklahoma. When a third wanderer joined them, they resolved to try to get up to Kansas to work in the fields.

In a somewhat confused sequence, Donaldson went on to relate how they had jumped on a passing train, where the brakeman demanded fifty cents from each of them for the ride. They threw him off, but he was able to jump aboard again on the caboose. Gunplay ensued (although no hints about how their guns were acquired), the law officers rode up and ordered their surrender. With their hands up, Williams snatched the pistol out of Donaldson's hands and began firing once more, killing the deputy constable. At that point, Donaldson and the remaining accomplice fled the scene.

He declared the story to be true and advised boys to stay at home and stay out of trouble. He saw no livelihood in the life of a hobo and that there was a job for every man eventually. At this point, Fred Donaldson leaves this narrative.

~~~

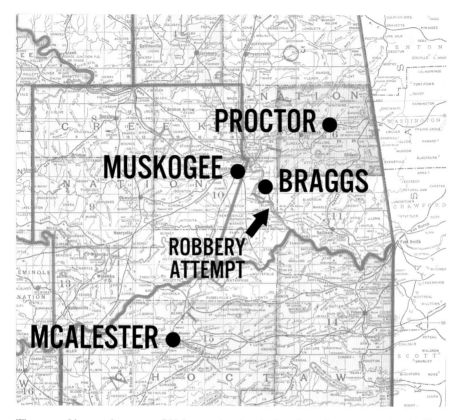

The area of interest in eastern Oklahoma, showing the locations of events associated with the failed train robbery by Paul Williams (Jesse Walker) and his accomplices in 1909. A new penitentiary had just been established in McAlester. Premier Series Map of Oklahoma and Indian Territory (detail) *(Chicago: Geographical Publishing Co., 1905); Library of Congress.*

In a couple of weeks, Williams was recovered enough to be arraigned and scheduled for trial in November 1909. Lacking counsel, a local judge was appointed to represent him, and he mounted a vigorous defense, despite the clarity of the crime. In a bit of drama, the guns used in the crime, still loaded, were placed on the evidence table in the courtroom—almost within reach of the defendant. The presiding judge was startled by this incautious action and ordered them removed at once. Donaldson, as the state's witness, reiterated his earlier story and claimed no knowledge of the identity of the constables, thinking they were another pair of hold-up men coming to interfere. As before, blame for the shoot-out was directed squarely at Williams.

In a quick trial, Williams was found guilty of manslaughter and bound over in November 1909 to serve a sentence of thirty years at the Oklahoma State Penitentiary at McAlester, about sixty miles away by train. He was booked in as prisoner number 1429, according to later correspondence from the warden (*Wilmington Morning Star*, March 21, 1915).

Once Williams arrived at McAlester and joined over one thousand other convicts there, he would have found a busy scene. Oklahoma had just begun the major construction phase of its new penitentiary complex. Until that time, prisoners from Oklahoma had been transported to Kansas. An Oklahoma-led investigation had found abysmal conditions there, along with questionable practices in the financial relationships between the two states.

After the preliminary construction of a stockade (and, later, an electric fence) to enclose temporary confinement buildings and the site, hundreds of Oklahoma prisoners were transported back from Kansas and set to

The Oklahoma State Penitentiary in McAlester was built by convicts between 1909 and 1912. The facility was intended to house most of the inmates in state custody, who, until that point, had been held in Kansas. The complex of buildings was surrounded by twenty-foot-high stone walls that presented a formidable barrier to escape. *Photograph courtesy of Oklahoma Historical Society.*

work on the 1,500-acre parcel. Throughout 1909, the area was cleared and graded, with the assistance of hundreds of pounds of dynamite that blasted through bedrock and teams of mules that hauled it away. By the time Williams arrived in early 1910, the prison's population was crowded into a modest complex of temporary facilities, but progress was being made on an enormous concrete wall to enclose about 10 acres of space for the permanent buildings.

Warden Robert W. Dick of the Oklahoma State Penitentiary. He was in charge when Paul Williams (Jesse Walker) was incarcerated in 1909 and assigned to work crews that were building the facility. Several years later, he played another role in Walker's exploits. *Photograph courtesy of Oklahoma Historical Society.*

Being young and presumably able-bodied after recovering from his wounds, Williams was likely assigned to well-guarded work gangs, where he got to know many veterans of the Kansas system and heard much about how bad things could get. At the direction of contractors and paid supervisors, these gangs arduously erected walls, installed cells and bars, fitted up stairwells and doors, painted and generally worked to build quarters that would confine them once again. Warden Robert W. Dick noted that, despite the nature of the work, there was "a spirit of camaraderie prevailing all about, and usually, the prisoners are congenial among themselves and, after all, have some pleasure, such as it is," (*Daily Ardmorite*, September 25, 1910).

Oklahoma took the penal approach of centralizing most of its prisoner population in the penitentiary, and the operation was supplemented by a prison farm outside the walls. Some prisoners were sent out to work camps to build roads, and others labored in a quarry to extract and dress stone for the new penitentiary. At the main site, some industries were established to manufacture uniforms and shoes, bedding, laundry services and the like. Two cellhouses were built for a capacity of about 1,200 prisoners, with allowances made to double that confinement capacity sometime in the future.

It did not take long for the confinement to be tested. In January 1914, three convicts feigned a desire to take care of some clerical business in the administrative building. Somehow, they had secured a handgun, and once they were in an office, they held the staff at bay and obtained keys to the outer doors. Using a couple of staff members as human shields, they made their way under fire to the outer gate in the wall. By issuing threats of harm to their hostages, they forced the guards to drop their firearms and open the gate. After commandeering a horse cart, they ditched the hostages and drove off. Close pursuit eventually pinned them down, and they were killed.

Word gets around quickly in prisons, and it was not long before Williams heard about the escape and how it was done. Only a couple of months later in 1914, he planned his own escape, perhaps from an assignment working the farm outside the walls. Trains passing on the nearby tracks of the Missouri, Kansas and Texas Railroad would have been a siren song to him, and one day, he bolted and likely hooked a ride away from the area.

And that was the end of Paul Williams—or was it?

8

WHAT GOES AROUND, COMES AROUND

t was March 5, 1915, and another spring was just around the corner in Wilmington, North Carolina. The dogwoods and azaleas had not quite budded out for their annual show, and the trees were just awakening to the longer days and warmer weather. The dredge *Henry Bacon* was leisurely working downstream on the Cape Fear River, making sure a sufficiently deep channel was in place for the ships berthing at Wilmington's busy waterfront wharves and piers. A motor launch shuttled crews and supplies back and forth between the dredge and the foot of Princess Street on the waterfront.

The *Wilmington Morning Star*, *Winston-Salem Western Sentinel*, *Greenville Eastern Reflector* and *New Bern Weekly Journal*.

On this Friday afternoon, young Frank Leonard, now about twenty years old, was working on the launch when the unwelcome appearance of Jesse Walker turned his next couple of days upside down. After a six-year absence, the fugitive from 1909 had come back to the area. He had apparently been with relatives in Columbus County for some time and then made his way down to lower Brunswick County and back up to Wilmington. Likely playing on familial associations (Walker had married Leonard's sister) and some contrived story about wanting to make amends, he finagled Leonard into taking him over to the dredge to find a job.

Whatever expectations Walker had about his prospects, it was an unsuccessful trip, and he returned with Leonard in the launch, which they tied up and there spent the night. On Saturday morning, Walker was determined to somehow get back down to Shallotte to connect with his family, a trip of some thirty miles. He had to press his case with his brother-in-law, but he eventually won Leonard over to his view.

A degraded candid photograph from the time shows the pair clowning around like a couple of tough guys, cigars clamped at the corners of their mouths. A *Wilmington City Directory* from the time lists several studios within a block of where they tied up the boat; perhaps they indulged in a bit of impulsive tomfoolery to celebrate Walker's plan. According to the *Wilmington Dispatch* (March 8, 1915), the two prepared for the trip, although Leonard was unenthusiastic about the venture.

> *Saturday afternoon, they rented bicycles from the Queen City Bicycle Company and started for Shallotte so Walker could see his wife and child. Young Leonard feigned illness when they had gone about five miles and told Walker that if he would return to Wilmington, he would get an automobile and take him to Shallotte. After getting back, they decided it was too late to make the trip, so they stayed aboard the launch Saturday night.*

On Sunday, the pair went to lunch at one of the several restaurants near their boat. By unfortunate coincidence, a boat captain from the Brunswick County town of Supply also happened to be eating there, and he recognized Walker and recalled the events from six years earlier. The captain immediately sought out authorities, and a warrant was drawn up by Justice of the Peace George Harriss. He assembled a posse of six city and county officers and drew up a plan for Walker's apprehension.

Meanwhile, according to the *Wilmington Dispatch* (March 8, 1915), Walker and Leonard returned to the launch to determine their next moves. They considered a new attempt to get down to Shallotte, this time with a rented automobile—if one could be found on Sunday. There was a car rental agency a few blocks away from their boat, and they perhaps thought they could take a car out for the day. Justice Harriss devised a ruse and somehow got word to Leonard that authorities were aware of Walker's presence and were arranging to have the launch fired upon by the nearby coast guard cutter *Seminole* that was berthed nearby.

Walker and Leonard were temporarily taken in by the story, and they scanned the shoreline for any signs of uniformed officers. Seeing none and dismissing their caution, they brazenly strolled ashore, perhaps to find some alternate place of refuge. The men of the posse were in plainclothes, however, and they proceeded to the streets near the river and kept an eye out for the two. When Walker was spotted, the officers nonchalantly posed as strolling pedestrians until they encountered their quarry. Casually separating to each side of him, two of the officers quickly pinned Walker's arms, while others immediately closed in to the front and behind him with guns drawn. The posse would later split a reward of about $500 for the arrest.

Walker offered no resistance; surprisingly, he seemed to have expected the apprehension. He was relieved of two handguns, an old-fashioned Colt .45 revolver and a Savage .32-caliber semi-automatic pistol. He readily admitted to his identity and stated at the outset that he had come back out of love for his wife and daughter. Once in custody, Walker was more thoroughly searched, yielding ammunition cartridges, a few small penknives, a handful of small change and some crude skeleton keys (the man loved his keys). He also had some letters, which he hastily destroyed before they could be secured; apparently, he had somehow been in correspondence with his wife. This suggests that at some point during his absence, he was in one place long enough to send and receive letters.

New Hanover County Sheriff S.P. Cowan took custody of Walker to await further disposition. In a jailhouse interview the next day, Walker was already embroidering his account with a reporter. The writer of the story in the *Wilmington Dispatch* (March 8, 1915) was surprised that someone who had been established as a dangerous desperado presented such a ready smile and agreeable manner. Walker had apparently kept his disarming ways, putting on a face of sincerity as he hinted at being a victim of circumstances.

Walker was relieved of two handguns when he was apprehended in Wilmington in 1915. One was an old Colt .45-caliber revolver (*top*), a weapon that was instantly recognizable and commanded respect. The other was a Savage .32-caliber automatic pistol (*bottom*), a useful "pocket pistol" that was easily concealed. *icollector.com.*

Word had been gotten out to Brunswick County Sheriff J.E. Robinson, and in due time, he arrived to take custody of the prisoner so that he could be transferred to Southport Jail. Walker now tried to wheedle himself out of this transfer with claims that it would be unfair and that it would probably lead to trouble. He declared that he had been mistreated there and did not want to repeat the experience. His pleas were to no avail. Sheriff Robinson had been a witness to Jackson Stanland's murder in 1908; indeed, he had been slightly wounded when Walker began firing wildly. He was not about to be swayed by any appeal to sympathy.

Continuing with the newspaper interview, Walker said that he had returned on his own volition to stand trial for the killing of Sheriff Stanland. "I've been in hell for six years," he said, "and I'm tired of it. I've come back to stand trial, and all I ask is a square deal." Showing some defiance, Walker named Irving B. Tucker, an attorney in Whiteville, to vouch for his intentions. A passing mention in a report suggests that an uncle of Walker's had helped make that arrangement. He also claimed that his apprehension had been prearranged, or even a frame-up, perhaps a nod to the ruse of the threat from the coast guard cutter. And then he hinted at some hasty half-baked plot to turn himself in voluntarily to the custody of Frank Leonard so that his brother-in-law could claim the reward money.

Walker only admitted to several days of reconnoitering. He claimed to have traveled to South America, Australia and other places in his six-year absence. If this claim triggers a memory, the reader might recall the written statement of one the accomplices in the failed train hold-up described previously—Walker may have appropriated it for his own purposes. And then, perplexingly, he preemptively emphasized that he did not kill a man in Oklahoma.

Walker in 1915, after being arrested in Wilmington. Newspapers had much to report on from his six-year absence after escaping from the Southport Jail. *Drawing from a newspaper photograph by Mitchell Henderson, His Lead Studio; author's collection, 2022.*

However, the young Leonard suggested that Walker had been skulking around in the vicinity for at least a few weeks. The Robinson family's memories suggest that he had holed up with kinfolk in Columbus County—thus the reference to a Whiteville attorney—for some time to recoup from traveling and to get some decent clothes. Then he made his way down to lower Brunswick County, where he hid for some days with a prominent family of his acquaintance. They were justifiably nervous about his presence there, even if he did claim a desire to see his wife and daughter. Rather than continuing to harbor the fugitive, they disinvited him in short order.

It was determined that Walker would be sent to Southport to be confined in the jail there. He again raised objections to the transfer, alleging previous mistreatment, but he was in no position to negotiate. That would be his destination until further actions could be arranged. Attorney W.J. Bellamy of Wilmington was retained as the counsel for Walker's defense. Right away, he raised the possibility that Sheriff Stanland's fatal visit in 1908 had been made without a valid warrant, perhaps setting the stage for a range of objections to the prosecution for that deed. A call was also made to the Whiteville attorney to join the defense.

On March 8, Walker was cuffed and shackled and led out through a crowd of about one hundred curious people who had gathered to see the central character in the drama that had unfolded years before. With Walker in the custody of Brunswick County sheriff Robinson and two deputies, the group shouldered their way through the excited throng to a waiting car for the trip to Southport. Now the center of attention, Walker seized the moment to sermonize a bit: "Never put a gun in your hand," he cried. "It will only lead to trouble." It was an obvious sentiment to state, but he had an audience.

In a few days, it was hinted by Walker's defense counsel that a change of venue would be sought. W.J. Bellamy cited Walker's fractious relationship with a reputable and well-known family in Brunswick County (the Leonards), the notorious nature of the case as it had been publicized in the press and the difficulty in empaneling an impartial jury, which is not difficult to imagine. The tragic circumstances of the Stanland family were also well known. A local minister visited Walker in jail and agreed to read a letter he had written at the church. The text was printed in the *Wilmington Morning Star* (March 16, 1915) and read as follows:

> *To my Christian friends of Southport:*
>
> *I am a victim of circumstances and need your help in many ways, especially your prayers. I have once been as you are, a Christian, and I am very anxious to regain the blessing. I desire the prayers of every Christian throughout this and other civilized counties.*
>
> *After being the supposed cause of so much excitement, I feel somewhat embarrassed, but when a man is down is when he needs help. Would to God that I could place my heart before you as a newspaper that you might see and read for yourself my every intent of desire in life, for God knows that I am not the black-hearted villain you have me pictured.*
>
> *I have come back to hear my fate, let it be good or bad. Gentlemen, I feel that someday I shall be a free man again: be in a position to prove by my every walk in life that I am not altogether the demon you have declared me to be. Let us pray for light to see that we may know best to do throughout the remaining days of our life.*

Whatever expectations Walker may have had for this appeal are unclear. Sheriff Stanland's widow had died from physical and psychological stress just three years after him. The seven Stanland children, now orphaned, had been taken in by the late sheriff's business partners in an arrangement that was unsympathetic and unwholesome. Walker had never established himself as a reputable citizen or good father, and the Leonard family was likely embarrassed to be associated with him. Finally, there is no acknowledgement in the letter of what he had done, much less any sense of remorse or regret. The appeal for thoughts and prayers, common enough even back then, were unlikely to have any impact. On March 15, after arguments were heard from both sides in a fully filled courtroom in Southport, the case was ordered to Pender County.

It was time to face the music.

9

A CONFLUENCE OF COINCIDENCES

A short time later, a chain of events unfolded that was emblazoned in a lengthy headline in the *Wilmington Morning Star* (March 21, 1915): "Circumstances Stranger Than Fiction Form Latest Development in Case of Man Who Killed Sheriff Stanland in 1908."

Dr. J.J. Johnson was on his way from Galveston, Texas, to Fort Caswell, near Southport, to assume medical duties there as an army surgeon. While riding the train into Wilmington, he read a newspaper account of Walker's recent arrest. He also noted Walker's unsolicited denial of killing someone in Oklahoma and some news about local authorities following up on that tidbit.

By coincidence, Dr. Johnson remembered that as a young doctor, he had attended to a gunman's wounds in Braggs, Oklahoma, following an attempted train robbery and shoot-out in 1909. In the trial following that incident, Dr. Johnson had testified against the assailant, Paul Williams, who was subsequently sent to the penitentiary to serve a thirty-year sentence for manslaughter. He did not know until that time that Williams had escaped from Oklahoma and might somehow be connected to Jesse Walker.

Dr. Johnson arrived in Wilmington and boarded the afternoon train of the Wilmington, Brunswick and Southern Railroad for the hour-and-a-half trip to Southport and assignment at Fort Caswell. He struck up a conversation with a fellow passenger about the Walker story and was then introduced to Brunswick County Sheriff Robinson, who, by coincidence, was on the same train. The doctor proceeded to relate his experiences in the 1909 incident, in which he treated a Paul Williams.

By coincidence, Sheriff Robinson had just been advised by his counterpart in New Hanover County about communication from Warden Robert W. Dick at the Oklahoma Penitentiary. That official described some independent investigative work that had been going on from afar, as quoted in the *Wilmington Morning Star* (March 21, 1915). With Walker confined in his jail, Sheriff Robinson recalled the message from Oklahoma:

> *Through McGilvray's Detective Agency, of Hattiesburg, Miss., I have been informed that you have in your jail Paul Williams, our no. 1429. He tells us that you have him upon a charge of murder committed in or near Southport and that he was going under the name of Jesse Walker. I am enclosing, herewith, his photo and description, and if he is our man and the evidence there isn't strong enough to convict him, be sure and notify us and we will gladly pay a reward of $50 for delivery to an officer of this institution. Please keep us posted about this matter, and if we can be of any service to you, command.*

Once they arrived in Southport, Sheriff Robinson and Dr. Johnson headed over to the jail, just down the block from the train station. Perhaps the sheriff devised a ruse of merely bringing a guest to show off his famous prisoner, an approach that would have appealed to Walker. The sheriff brought Dr. Johnson to see Walker, and they probably had a bit of conversation. After the visit, the sheriff asked the doctor if Walker was the man he had treated. The doctor identified Walker as the Paul Williams he had seen in Oklahoma, and he proceeded to describe the wounds that had been treated.

The next day, Sheriff Robinson brought an officer down from Wilmington, and together, they paid another visit to Walker. He was ever the talkative type, and they engaged him in conversation and got him to show off his wounds. He claimed he received them while escaping the manhunt in the Green Swamp years before, when he had been shot at by a posse. However, the location and nature of the wounds precisely matched what the doctor had described earlier.

The sheriff now had a match to the photograph and description sent by the Oklahoma penitentiary warden. He also had a positive identification from the doctor who had been at the aftermath of the train robbery and shoot-out and a confirmation of the doctor's recollections with an actual witnessed observation of the wounds on Walker's body. Based on this evidence, it was deemed sufficient in those times to conclude that Jesse Walker and Paul Williams were one and the same man. Fingerprint comparisons were still some years away, and DNA matching, of course, was beyond anyone's conception. Documents were updated, communications were sent out and preparations for the trial began in earnest.

W.J. Bellamy, Walker's defense counsel, immediately denounced the findings in the *Wilmington Morning Star* (March 21, 1915). He stated his position that Walker had never been in Oklahoma, that stories to that effect were pure fiction and that the evidence provided was just a series of "manufactured facts," adjusted to fit the circumstances—in today's parlance, a collection of untrustworthy "fake news." He also saw such revelations as prejudicial to his client's case and urged a speedy removal to Pender County. If such sentiments sound familiar, they can still be heard from defense counsels at sensational trials today. The attorney's words were quoted in the newspaper article:

> *There* [Pender County], *Walker, in accord with his counsel's views, free from prejudice, venom, hatred and hardness of heart can be tried fairly, impartially and justly by jurors who will be governed not by prejudice and passion, but by the evidence and the law of the land....Walker himself, counseled and comforted by the fact that he will now have an impartial trial, has nothing to fear; imbued with a faith that when the people shall finally hear the whole truth, he will stand in the eyes of the law and the opinion of all honest men, free and fully vindicated of the charge—the unfortunate victim of a frame-up—in law, in truth and fact—an innocent man.*

Following through on his prediction that incarceration in Southport would lead to trouble, Walker lost little time in becoming a quarrelsome inmate. He lodged various complaints about the conditions of his confinement and generally groused about the treatment he was receiving. He had somehow managed to carve a couple of wooden false keys (keys, again!) and tried to enlist help to attempt another escape. In short, he was not doing himself any favors—but facing a murder trial, what did he have to lose?

The trial date for Walker's case was set for the May 31 session of the Pender County Superior Court in Burgaw, where it was entered as part of the regular docket. Sessions were held only once every three months, and there were over one hundred other cases to be heard, but Walker's appearance was certainly the most anticipated. About two hundred men had been summoned for a jury pool, from which twelve would be selected to sit in judgment. Many witnesses were also waiting, having been called from Brunswick County and other areas to testify in the case.

The Pender County Courthouse before 1936. Walker's case was heard here in 1915, resulting in him being sentenced to thirty years in jail. A not guilty plea to a lesser charge of manslaughter kept him from the electric chair. *Photograph courtesy of Pender County Library.*

Judge George Rountree was to hear the case at the Pender County Courthouse. Hints in news stories about the trial (*Wilmington Morning Star*, June 1, 1915) suggest that Rountree was a no-nonsense jurist. He typically aimed for quick dispatch of the cases brought before him and was not one to tolerate a lot of argument. Given the length of the docket, it was easy to predict a quick pace for dispositions. There was another murder trial scheduled, along with a host of angry farmers with citations for violating a newly enacted law governing the control of livestock. It was his order to recruit two hundred men to form the jury pool for Walker's case, and selection was bound to be a drawn-out affair. As it was stated in the dry language of jurisprudence:

> *In obedience to the foregoing order at 2 o'clock p.m. in the presence of J.B. Davis, register of deeds, His Honor George Rountree, judge presiding, Homer L. Lyons, solicitor, the prisoner J.C. Walker with his attorney D.H. Beard Esq. being present, a special venire of two hundred men were drawn to report at the courthouse in Burgaw at 2 o'clock p.m. Wednesday, June 2nd, 1915.*

Walker's defense team consisted of W.J. Bellamy of Wilmington and Irving B. Tucker of Whiteville. For some reason, they were absent without explanation for the morning session, so the jury question was postponed until the afternoon. When counsel did not show up then either, the judge dispatched some fiery telegrams and named a substitute attorney, D.H. Beard, for the jury drawing and other pretrial matters. Walker's attorneys likely got their affairs in order promptly, pleading for forbearance while they finished preparations.

Indications are that they were mounting an aggressive defense and entered a not guilty plea. They alleged, among other things, that the original arrest warrants to be served by Sheriff Jackson Stanland had some defects, that the sheriff had improperly entered the dwelling where Walker was staying, that Walker was taken by surprise with no notice and simply reacted in self-defense and that the warrants for relatively minor offenses did not justify the intimidating show of force used to serve them. There was a further detail that would have a greater effect.

Judge Rountree was well aware of the notoriety of the case and the unwelcome attention it was getting in his courtroom. He was looking at a protracted jury selection and dozens of witnesses—mostly for the prosecution, to be lengthily cross-examined by defense. The trial would be held in a courtroom crowded with spectators, press coverage and all the drama of a death penalty trial that might drag on for some time. All of it would go on at significant expense to the county and in the summer heat—air conditioning was still decades away. Judge Rountree directed the prosecution and defense teams to confer with each other and reach an agreement on how to proceed with the case.

In a pretrial hearing, Brunswick County Sheriff J.E. Robinson and two others presented their testimonies about the case, solidly establishing that the crime of homicide had been committed and verifying the identities of the victim and perpetrator. While such testimony was unchallenged, Walker's attorneys brought forward the detail that led to an important change. They pointed out that

Superior court judge George Rountree, who presided over Walker's trial in 1915 that sent him to the North Carolina Central Prison in Raleigh. Twenty years later, he would comment in favor of a pardon for Walker. *Image from* History of North Carolina, *vol. 4 (Chicago: Lewis Publishing Company, 1919).*

there was no premeditation in committing the crime, given the sudden and impulsive circumstances surrounding it. This would have been a key item to prove in the proffered charge of murder in the first degree.

The judge ordered the defense counsels to confer with prosecutors and come back with a recommendation. The basic facts in the case were not in dispute—Walker had fatally shot the sheriff in front of witnesses, all of which could be conclusively proven. Excuses about the technicalities of the case (taken by surprise, unseemly show of force, self-defense, et cetera) were unlikely to sway a jury from what might be a foregone verdict. If the prosecution wanted to proceed with a lengthy trial for first-degree murder, there was the possibility it might fail in the absence of premeditation, or if it succeeded, it would be overturned on appeal.

Having a proven crime in hand, the lawyers crafted a solution in the interests of expediency. A guilty plea to a lesser charge could move the trial along much more quickly, would not require a jury and could wrap the case up promptly. It is not known who was paying for Walker's defense—a passing note in a report mentioned an uncle in Georgia—but many expensive hours of representation would have been required for a full court trial. Some discussion with Walker was required, and his lawyers managed to persuade him to go along with the deal. After all, he would be certain to avoid the electric chair. As recorded in minutes of the trial:

> *The defendant being present at the bar of the court…and having previously been arraigned in open court and pleaded not guilty of the felony and murder whereof he stands charged, whereupon the prisoner through his said counsel tendered to the state a plea of not guilty of murder in the first degree but guilty of murder in the second degree, which is accepted by the solicitor.*

The plea was submitted to Judge Rountree, who approved it, possibly thankful to avoid the more drawn-out process of a full trial. Potential jurors and witnesses were notified that their appearance would not be required, and they were dismissed. Likewise, witnesses were notified that they would not be testifying; there may have been some disappointment at the news. Walker was immediately sentenced to thirty years imprisonment at the Central State Prison in Raleigh. After some final paperwork, Sheriff Robinson and a Pender County deputy, L.Q. Myers, bundled Walker into a car and drove him the one hundred or so miles to Raleigh, where he was admitted to the Central State Prison.

It wouldn't be much of a sightseeing trip.

10

GO TO JAIL, GO DIRECTLY TO JAIL

PART TWO

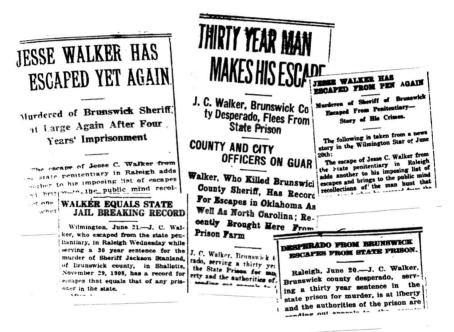

JESSE WALKER HAS ESCAPED YET AGAIN

Murdered of Brunswick Sheriff: at Large Again After Four Years' Imprisonment

The escape of Jesse C. Walker from the state penitentiary in Raleigh adds another to his imposing list of escapes and brings to the public mind recollections when

WALKER EQUALS STATE JAIL BREAKING RECORD

Wilmington, June 21.—J. C. Walker, who escaped from the state penitentiary, in Raleigh Wednesday while serving a 30 year sentence for the murder of Sheriff Jackson Stanland, of Brunswick county, in Shallotte, November 29, 1908, has a record for escapes that equals that of any prisoner in the state.

THIRTY YEAR MAN MAKES HIS ESCAPE

J. C. Walker, Brunswick County Desperado, Flees From State Prison

COUNTY AND CITY OFFICERS ON GUARD

Walker, Who Killed Brunswick County Sheriff, Has Record For Escapes in Oklahoma As Well As North Carolina; Recently Brought Here From Prison Farm

J. C. Walker, Brunswick County desperado, serving a thirty year sentence in the State Prison for murder, and the authorities of

JESSE WALKER HAS ESCAPED FROM PEN AGAIN

Murderer of Sheriff of Brunswick Escaped From Penitentiary— Story of His Crimes.

The following is taken from a news story in the Wilmington Star of June 20th:

The escape of Jesse C. Walker from the State penitentiary in Raleigh adds another to his imposing list of escapes and brings to the public mind recollections of the man hunt that

DESPERADO FROM BRUNSWICK ESCAPES FROM STATE PRISON.

Raleigh, June 20.—J. C. Walker, Brunswick county desperado, serving a thirty year sentence in the state prison for murder, is at liberty and the authorities of the prison are sending out appeals to the

I nstead of carrying on the life of a vagabond, Walker now had to settle into the regimented lifestyle of a prison convict. He was duly registered and numbered, issued a prison uniform and assigned to a cell for an evaluation period. With his background, some extra precautions may have been taken at first, and there were rules to be followed. At least there were predictable meals, shelter and no worries about pursuit (at least not yet). It is likely he once again fell into a pattern of amiable compliance, all the while registering little details about how things were run, getting to know the guards, putting in work hours and keeping his ears open.

Walker would have found this environment very different to the one he experienced during his earlier penal years in Oklahoma. For one thing, this prison had been in operation for many years, running under a system conceived during a period of social reform. This meant that, in theory, prisoners could be rehabilitated through principles of meaningful work, education and adequate facilities. In practice, however, there was no relief from the daily and constant reminders that they were in a punitive environment; indeed, the disciplinary "whipping post" was still a fixture that would not be abolished until 1922. With a pattern of good behavior, inmates might be able to earn a small amount of privilege. However, that could be removed with infractions against a somewhat arbitrary set of rules.

Walker would also have found out that the prison itself was never designed to handle all the convicts under state custody. Many prisoners were deployed to prison farms to cultivate provisions for the system and presumably acquire knowledge in agricultural practices. A majority of prisoners were leased out to counties around the state to work on various projects. Most often, these were road improvement projects, as the state was working hard to improve its network of highways. The intended goal was to operate as a self-sufficient system to minimize the tax burden on the good citizens of the state. Whatever veneer of social improvement was intended, the system was not far removed from slavery.

In his report from 1913, the prison superintendent noted that, of the 2,800 convicts under supervision, 2,000 were assigned to county road projects, housed in work camps and usually operated in chain gangs. Another 300 were working on railroad projects in similar circumstances. The remaining 500 prisoners housed at the central prison were mostly employed in prison industry activities. Among these prisoners were those who were too old to work, infirm or mentally incapable; incorrigible offenders; or part of the small group of female convicts. Remote prison farms held another several hundred inmates.

The idea of "working off" sentences might have been intended as a way to achieve some social benefit from criminals. However, the absence of a parole method was beginning to generate more prisoners under supervision than could be meaningfully deployed. Arrivals were simply coming into the system faster than the existing population could cycle out of their sentences. In addition, there were growing objections being raised from private contractors around the state about being cut out from road projects. In some years' time, the model would be revised to address these concerns, one method being to shorten sentences for good behavior and implementing a system of parole.

Good behavior is something Walker had practice at, and in time, he was able to participate in prison work assignments and integrate with the other inmates. Stir time is slow time, so it is said, and after a couple of years, Walker became restive within the boundaries of his prescribed world. Waking, sleeping, working, attending assemblies and mealtimes and passing between parts of the prison—all were regulated. And all of these things were rigorously defined by the everlasting numbering, counting and checking and the ever-present system of locks, bars and gates.

Four years into his thirty-year sentence, in 1919, Walker was chafing under the circumstances of his confinement. By this time, he had earned the "privilege" of being transferred to the Caledonia State Prison Farm, formerly a colonial-era plantation called Caledonia. This was about eighty miles to the east, near Halifax, North Carolina, along a bend of the Roanoke River. Along with several hundred other inmates, he worked on the seven-thousand-acre tract, where they grew crops and tended livestock,

The North Carolina Central Prison was situated just outside of Raleigh and was designed primarily for the minority of those inmates who could not be sent out to work on the prison farm, in road improvements and in railroad construction. *University of North Carolina at Chapel Hill Digital Collection.*

processed food and prepared it for distribution to other prison facilities and encampments around the state.

The farm may have seemed less confining than the stone walls of the central prison, but there was no mistaking its routine. A wooden stockade surrounded the grounds, prisoners were crowded into dormitories and guards regularly patrolled the area. Discipline was rigorously enforced. Walker had some issues with the conditions there, and he submitted complaints to the Prisoners Relief Society, a prison reform organization based in Washington, D.C. The organization's attention was particularly drawn to North Carolina, based on reports they were receiving.

Considering Walker's complaints, along with others from North Carolina, the Prisoners Relief Society promised an investigation. As might be expected, Governor Thomas W. Bickett was not about to allow outsiders any opportunity to inspect the state's prisons, with such declarations sometimes being made colorfully. It is entirely plausible that any prisoners who made complaints had their lives made more difficult. Walker's complaints were dismissed, and it may be that his reactions were an unwelcome distraction to the discipline of the farm. Reforms were indeed made but would come almost a decade later.

North Carolina governor Thomas W. Bickett, who resisted investigations of the state prison system in the late 1910s and early 1920s. Later reforms significantly improved the conditions of the state's prisons and the character of imprisonment. *Photograph courtesy of the Library of Congress.*

It is unknown if Walker established any record of correspondence while he was imprisoned. There are earlier instances of him having written to certain parties, and he had been apprehended in 1915 with letters in his possession—although he quickly destroyed them. It is also unknown if he received any visits from his wife or relatives, however awkward they might have been. It would have been a bit of a trip by automobile, even if the roads were improving across the state. By train, it would have been more complicated, requiring a couple of transfers to different trains between southeastern North Carolina and Raleigh.

Somewhere along the line, Walker probably learned that his eleven-year-old daughter, Clara Lee, had died in October 1918. The Robinson family's recollections suggest that

Rosa Lee Walker and her daughter Clara Lee in formal sittings circa 1917. Clara Lee would die in 1918 from scarlet fever, according to Leonard family memories. *Photographs courtesy of J.R. Robinson, Robinson family history.*

the cause of her death was scarlet fever, a common childhood peril of the time and one that was seen frequently during those years. A later notation on her death certificate indicates her cause of death was pneumonia, complicated by influenza, and she could have been one of the millions of victims of the great pandemic that occurred during that time. Walker would not be allowed to return to Shallotte for funeral observances, and that may have rankled him. He may have sought and been denied a short furlough for bereavement, but he had to stay put.

In any event, Walker's troublesome behavior, at some point, stood out enough that he was transferred back to the main prison in Raleigh, "on account of restlessness," according to the *Wilmington Morning Star* (June 20, 1919). It should be recalled that this was the guy who had made assertions about not being taken alive, burning down the woods and even reportedly declaring vengeance on his father-in-law, whom he blamed for tipping off the sheriff before the 1908 shooting. Perhaps this was just reckless talk and hollow boasting, but people remembered.

The 1918 death certificate of Clara Lee, Walker's daughter by Rosa Lee. A later notation said she died from pneumonia, with influenza as the contributing cause. Only eleven years old, Rosa Lee died at home without medical care. Walker himself was at the North Carolina Central Prison in Raleigh at the time. *Register of Deeds, Brunswick County, North Carolina.*

Whatever restlessness Walker felt, he found an outlet in June 1919. During or just after his leisure time in the main yard of the central prison among the other inmates, Walker, it was reported, managed to make another escape. It would not be until the next day, however, that his absence was noted. At first, it was thought that he had somehow found a secret hiding place among the prison buildings, but a thorough search yielded nothing. Then the possibility was floated that he had acquired civilian clothes and made an exit among visitors. Such a method would have raised uncomfortable questions about security, but those apparently went unanswered.

It finally had to be acknowledged that Walker had once again managed to get away. Newspaper articles highlighted the escape, reminding people, once again, about Walker's backstory and history of offenses. A letter mailed from Fayetteville was delivered to the Brunswick County sheriff. In it, Walker asked for the return of the two guns he had been relieved of in 1915—a rather nervy request, considering the situation. Another letter was sent to the officer in charge of the prison farm, in which he requested that some of his personal belongings be sent to kinfolk in Columbus County. A reward of $325 was offered for Walker's capture, a value well over $5,000 today. At the end of it all, though, it seemed as though he had simply disappeared.

He was off on another adventure.

11

IN THE MAGNOLIA STATE

At this point in the narrative, we enter a "dark period," one that is only hinted at through small bits and pieces dropped into other later stories. A plausible storyline can be composed, but for about a decade, there is precious little to be found by way of a documented foundation. I ask for your indulgence as I engage in some authorial license.

Sometime in the late summer of 1919, Frank Manning dropped off the freight train of the Mobile and Ohio Railroad around Crawford, Mississippi. Just a small upstate town of maybe three hundred souls, Crawford was surrounded by farms, with cotton as its main cash crop, along with fields of sorghum, peas, corn, wheat and other foodstuffs. Livestock grazed the fields and hedgerows, nibbling at whatever they could find of any leafy forage. There were still forested tracts in the area, along with lumber operations. Harvest season was already underway, and Manning figured this would be as good a place as any to set for a while and see if he could hire himself out.

He was in time for the season; other transients were already rolling through the area to augment the local workforce. The country was experiencing a brief depression as it adjusted to circumstances following World War I, and millions of army veterans had been discharged. As production needs wound down in the peacetime economy, there was nowhere near the demand for workers as there had been. Hundreds of thousands of men (and a small fraction of women) were riding the rails, migrating around, looking for any opportunity to earn some money.

Walker (under the name Frank C. Manning) drifted into the area around Crawford, Mississippi, in 1920. There, he met and married seventeen-year-old Frances Britt, who was twenty years younger than he was. *Photograph courtesy of the Interstate Commerce Commission, valuation reports.*

Seasonal occupations, like agriculture, offered temporary possibilities during planting and harvest times.

Glad to stay put for a spell, Manning may have found the remains of a hobo camp near the tracks and decided to stake out the place. A stroll into town might have yielded some handouts or maybe even a job that included food and shelter. His appearance was travel-rough but really not much worse than that of most of the dirt farm folks in the area or others who showed up looking for work. He might have been able to get some decent clothes, too; he knew he was a smooth talker and could probably persuade someone out of some serviceable secondhands or castoffs, especially shoes.

Just a few miles to the south, along the tracks, was Brooksville. This was a somewhat larger town with businesses, warehouses and more opportunities for employment. There, he met young Frances Britt, only seventeen years old, twenty years his junior. With his life experiences, Frank probably had a lot to say, regaling her with tales of travel and exciting glimpses of the wider world. Before long, they were married in Crawford in 1920 in what would have been a small ceremony. Frank hinted at some dark misdeeds in his past, but there was no serious discussion of what these things were—such tales may have been a common trait among itinerants. Frances was apparently content to let things be, likely satisfied that she had a husband.

At some point, the couple decided to move on, probably at Frank's instigation. He did not seem to be one to attach himself to a place for very long, and there might have been some possibilities he wanted to explore. According to later accounts, the pair packed up their few belongings and went twenty-five miles up the road to West Point for a while. A shared newspaper report said they moved to Houston, Texas—an arduous journey of over six hundred miles—perhaps because that was the only Houston of note to the writer. However, I find it far more likely that they moved to Houston, Mississippi, a mere thirty miles away in the next county over. Here, they would have lived in similar circumstances among dirt farms and cultural familiarity.

After a couple of years, they moved again, this time settling farther downstate in Meridian. Eventually, Frank and Frances Manning found their way down to Gulfport in 1926. There, they bought a modest house on Gulf Avenue, near the Louisville and Nashville Railroad tracks, just outside the city limits. Frank began putting himself out as a home-based craftsman and sometime jeweler. He apparently had some skills in fine mechanics and was adept at repairing clocks and watches, and he may have done a little locksmithing as well. He also bought and sold jewelry, sometimes door to door.

Gulfport had active shipping and maritime trades, and times were relatively good for a while. A population of about ten thousand grew up around the port facilities, and the lumber business was a major component of the local economic life. The bustling city was located about halfway between the much greater cities of New Orleans and Mobile, and railroads stretched to the east, north and west to keep Gulfport connected to the commerce of a growing collection of coastal communities.

Frank built up a group of friends and acquaintances, meeting them socially and going along on hunting and fishing trips to reinforce his relationships—in today's parlance, he began "networking." He also established a reputation as a fair and honest tradesman, friendly and talkative, often with a store of tales that hinted at some adventuresome exploits. In 1931, he was listed in the city directory as a "collector," although the definition of that occupation is unclear. It may have been nothing more than someone who would scavenge bits and pieces of discarded stuff around town.

The Great Depression fell on Gulfport, as it did everywhere else in the country, and Manning found it increasingly difficult to sustain his purported trade. A home garden helped with their food supply, and perhaps he began bartering services for other goods in lieu of hard cash. Such arrangements were not uncommon where jobs were scarce and income was unreliable. In those times of want and woe, however, he was compelled to go on relief to make ends meet. Frances picked up occasional work as a seamstress.

The Mannings also settled in with the local church going folk. Frank began attending services with Assembly of God and Church of the Nazarene congregations, maybe hedging his spiritual bets. Something about the evangelical traditions of these denominations must have resonated with him. Congregants were encouraged to seek grace to be justified with the Lord, and altar calls and testimonies were regular parts of services, which were held multiple times a week. For those so moved, their response would lead them to a point of a spiritual awakening and rebirth. This point of conversion led to a life of atonement and good works, along with efforts to avoid sinful behavior.

By some accounts, Manning experienced his epiphany in 1932. The Church of the Nazarene in Gulfport erected a tent and launched a series of revival meetings in January and February. Over the course of several weeks, crowds were welcomed to old-standard spiritual songs and tub-thumping favorites led by recruits from local church choirs. The central focus, of course, was the inspiring sermons. Some of the themes included "A Quick Way to Go to Hell," "Inevitable Result of Sin" and "Our Moral and Religious Debts," according to notices in the *Biloxi Sun Herald*. They were not the cheeriest of titles, perhaps, but they always encouraged listeners to find a means of redemption.

These tent services would often begin with some spirited gathering music ("There Is Power in the Blood" or "I Stand Amazed in the Presence," for example), followed by welcoming prayers and messages. More songs might follow ("Rescue the Perishing" or "Throw Out the Lifeline") to set the mood for a long and fervent message of hope and salvation. There would usually be an occasion for meeting-goers to come forward and testify or receive a special blessing (with more music, such as "Rock of Ages," "Sweet Hour of Prayer" or "Blessed Assurance"). Following an obligatory "pass-the-hat" offering, the service might close with a rousing send-off ("Leaning on the Everlasting Arms" or "Standing on the Promises"). On one of these occasions, Manning felt the call to mark a turning point in his life and was moved to respond. He also felt called to study the Bible and evangelize.

We do not know what inspired him, but Manning felt himself a new man, and, what's more, he was a man with a mission. As described by friends and acquaintances, he enthusiastically pursued a devout life and, more than ever, became a model citizen. Not yet fifty years old, his hair prematurely turned white, although he retained a youthful appearance and likeable manner. He was still caught up in financial hard times, though, and relied on modest government relief payments while Frances sought out odd jobs and took up sewing. He announced his plans to explore opportunities elsewhere and said he would send for her when something came up.

It was in the early spring of 1935 when Frank left Gulfport, stating that his aim was to find employment and get off relief rolls. He indicated that he was hitchhiking to Georgia to explore prospects. He told his wife he knew a minister there who might point him to some gainful employment. He took care to establish a garden at his home for Frances, since he expected not to return any time soon. She, unaware of his inner counsels, helped him pack for his trip and probably sent him off with affectionate wishes for good luck.

The country was in the grip of the Depression, and Manning likely drew on experience and stitched his trip together with stages on freight trains and hitchhiking. These were common enough ways to get around for those in need, and there were sympathetic drivers on the roads. He would be able to blend in with others in similar circumstances, possibly staying at hobo camps along the way. A few dollars in his pocket would help where meals or lodging were needed. It took him about two weeks to *not* arrive in Georgia.

Instead, he arrived in Raleigh, North Carolina, a trip of over eight hundred miles.

12

A CHAPTER OF REVELATIONS

O n a mild spring day in April 1935, a man approached a large building near the edge of Raleigh, North Carolina, having just been dropped off there by friends after a trip from Whiteville in Columbus County. He may have paused for a few moments on the road that led across the tracks of the Seaboard Air Line Railroad to consider his next moves. On the other side, behind a brick wall, lay a broad lawn, neatly bisected by the road he was walking, which led to what was obviously an administrative building.

Beyond the administrative building and to either side stood large wings of the structure, with the entire red brick mass topped by crenellations, turrets, cupolas and other embellishments of a Gothic style. Overall, the aspect was a forbidding one and with just cause. This was North Carolina's Central State Prison, completed in 1884. Stout iron bars stood in the windows overlooking the lawn. Out of sight behind the building was the main yard and its facilities, enclosed by a massive twenty-foot-high stone wall.

There was nothing remarkable about the man as he calmly checked in at the guard shelter at the front yard entrance. He strode to the building entrance and entered. He had a pleasant demeanor, was neatly dressed and his prematurely white hair belied his fifty-two years. He checked in again with the reception guard and announced his wish to see the warden. With permission granted, he walked into the warden's office and announced: "I've come back to get shed of my time, warden."

And so began the last stage of the remarkable life of Jesse C. Walker, the cop killer from Brunswick County, North Carolina, whose deed in 1908 launched an odyssey to Oklahoma and Mississippi before returning to the Tar Heel State. His exploits had generated hundreds of column inches in newspapers for more than three decades. For a time, his story was the biggest crime saga in North Carolina. Constructed from later reports, he had had a few more incidents occur before he showed up in Raleigh.

Walker had made it from Gulfport as far as Whiteville, North Carolina, where he stayed with people he knew for a couple of days. (He may have actually made a stopover in Georgia, where he purportedly had kinfolk.) According to the Stanland family's memories, he then went down to Shallotte, of all places. Here, he set about proclaiming his interpretation of saving grace at the Campground Methodist Church in the center of town. It is probably safe to assume that he had good intentions with his evangelism attempt. It attracted attention, but he undoubtedly stirred up unwelcome memories of encounters a couple decades earlier.

In another of those unfortunate coincidences, one of the sons of the late Sheriff Stanland was also in Shallotte for a brief stay. He was known to hold a deep and abiding resentment stemming from father's murder. After his mother died from grief, he and his orphaned siblings grew up as wards of his father's business partner under difficult circumstances. It can be appreciated that he would be eager to confront the source of that grief and seek redress. When Walker learned about the presence of this very personal

An aerial view of the North Carolina Central State Prison site. From the railroad tracks across the front of the property, one would proceed past a guardhouse and wall to the administration building, behind which was spread the cell houses. A twenty-foot-tall stone wall surrounded the main yard, which held occupational buildings and ancillary structures. *University of North Carolina at Chapel Hill Digital Collection.*

antagonist, he lost no time in suspending his evangelism and finding his way out of Shallotte. A rapid exit brought him back to the friendlier refuge of his relatives around Whiteville.

From there, plans were hastily made to launch Walker on the final leg of his journey to Raleigh. Aside from being motivated to atone for his earlier life—a matter of the spirit—there may have been a more practical desire to find a safe place away from the potentially vengeful actions of his victim's children. He was driven up to Raleigh and presented himself for reincarceration at the Central State Prison. His trek from Gulfport had taken about two weeks, according to his Mississippi neighbors who were contacted by the *Biloxi Daily Herald* (April 10, 1935).

Warden H.H. Honeycutt claimed to recognize him, according to a report (*Burlington Daily Times-News*, April 12, 1935), but he was somewhat incredulous that this could be the same man who had escaped confinement

Walker in 1935, when he voluntarily surrendered to the North Carolina Central State Prison after a sixteen-year absence. Officials had to dig into their records to refresh their memory about why he had been incarcerated in the first place. *Drawing from a newspaper photograph by Mitchell Henderson, His Lead Studio; author's collection, 2022.*

sixteen years earlier. Gone was the tough-guy bravado that had made Walker such a challenge to keep locked up. Indeed, it took a bit of an effort to dig up his records to figure out what he had been convicted of and his sentencing documents.

In short order, Walker went through a series of procedures that were much more elaborate than those of his incarceration twenty years earlier. He was bathed and disinfected, traded his street clothes for prison attire, met with the warden to be indoctrinated with the prison rules, was photographed and fingerprinted, provided information for a data profile, was sent to the prison physician and dentist for examinations and inoculations and returned to the warden's office for assignment. This process had been instituted in the 1920s, as described in the "Report of the State Prison Department" (1932).

When his registration was complete, Walker was assigned and escorted to a cell where he could settle in. He also received a work assignment. Unlike twenty years earlier, prisoners were no longer aggregated into a large labor pool for a random selection of jobs. Instead, some thought went into the assignments, considering age, education, physical condition, aptitudes and existing skills. These assessments were part of a wide-ranging series of reforms that had been instituted over the previous ten years. Walker's initial assignment was to join the crew that was remodeling the prison hospital, a desperately needed improvement. There would be no duties outside the walls this time.

Just after he turned himself in, Walker wrote to his second wife, Frances "Manning," telling her that he had been living under the alias of Frank Manning. He revealed his identity and his intentions to atone for past misdeeds. She had gotten hints that he had done some bad things shortly after they got married, but she remained largely ignorant of the details, since they had not discussed them at length. Undoubtedly, this letter was a shock. Recollections from the Leonard family—into which Walker had first married in 1905—suggest that he had chosen the easy-to-remember name of "Frank," as that was the name of his brother-in-law Frank Leonard. There are no clues about his choice of "Manning."

Not surprisingly, Frances was overcome by the letter, coming as it did after several weeks of no communication. The letter contained quite a list of revelations. In summary:

- The man she had known as Frank C. Manning for sixteen years was really Jesse C. Walker.
- He hadn't ended up to Georgia after all; he had gone to North Carolina.
- He was writing from the North Carolina Central State Prison.
- He turned himself in to complete a sentence for killing the Brunswick County sheriff in 1908.
- He still had twenty-six years left on his sentence.

It is unknown if he divulged that he had been married before (and divorced) with a deceased daughter. Even in a confessional letter, that may have been too much. He apparently also withheld his intention to eventually make amends in Oklahoma, leaving that unpleasant surprise for a later occasion.

Frances was comforted by her friends, but it was a heavy blow to have this past unloaded on her in such a way. After some quick deliberations, she packed up for a long absence, left the house to be tended by neighbors and moved to Raleigh. There, she could be close to her husband during the next phase of his affairs. Small jobs here and there sustained her until Walker's case could be resolved. In the middle of the Depression, jobs were not plentiful, but she managed to get herself established. Undoubtedly, there were visits to her husband, although there are no records of this.

Word quickly got around in Gulfport, and Walker's friends began organizing an appeal for clemency in recognition of his exemplary life while residing there. Testimonials and petitions were rapidly gathered from a circle of acquaintances and friends, all attesting to his life of upright behavior and decency. In his time in Gulfport, Walker had crossed paths with many people in the town, and his activism in the church, pursued with some fervor, bespoke his life as a model citizen. Even Mississippi governor M.S. Conner vouched for the legitimacy of the effort, as he forwarded the appeals to North Carolina.

Shortly thereafter, the children of the slain Sheriff Stanland got involved. Despite the long period since the commission of the crime—now twenty-six

MOST WANTED IN BRUNSWICK COUNTY

years—they vigorously opposed any form of clemency or parole. As printed in *The State Port Pilot* (June 12, 1935), their petition pointed out that, besides the loss of a father, their mother died of grief a few years later and they were effectively orphaned by Walker's crime. Had he not escaped and served at least a minimum term, they might be more favorably inclined toward his cause. However, the harm done, along with circumstances of an incomplete sentence, could not overcome whatever pleas of remorse he might have. The letter printed in the *State Port Pilot* laid out their case rather thoroughly.

> *New Britain, Connecticut*
> *June 3, 1935*
> *To His Excellency, J.C.B. Ehringhaus, governor of the State of North Carolina*
>
> *My dear governor,*
>
> *It has come to my attention, and that of my brothers and sisters, that one Jesse C. Walker, who shot my father, Jackson Stanland, about 25 or 26 years ago, has returned to the Central Prison at Raleigh, N.C., after having escaped more than 16 years ago, and that a petition is being drawn in his behalf for a pardon.*
>
> *Our family at the present time consists of seven children: Thomas, Chauncey, Herman, Edward, Bessie, Catherine and Murphy.*
>
> *At the time that Walker shot my father, there was an attempt to lynch him, and it was because of my father's insistence that he be given a fair trial that this was avoided. Before he came to trial, however, Walker escaped and was not apprehended for about five or six years. Subsequent thereto, he was sentenced to thirty years in the Central Prison. After having served four or five years, he escaped and has now returned.*
>
> *As a result of my father's death, our mother's heart was broken, and she died three years after my father. We were seven orphans and had pretty hard struggling during the years when we were young. We lost our father and mother, and we feel that Walker, whom we understand in the first instance was an army deserter and against whom five warrants were out at the time my father attempted to make the arrest and did not serve his sentence and fulfill his debt to society.*
>
> *My brothers, sisters and I have given this matter serious consideration and thought if this man had served a minimum of the sentence, at least, we would be glad to sign a petition for a pardon, but in view of his escape and*

his failure to serve anywhere near the sentence which was rendered, and the suffering that we children have had as a result of the shooting of my father, prompts us to send this petition to you opposing the executive clemency.

H.A. Stanland

The wheels of the justice and corrections system slowly turned. In a few weeks, Walker, through legal counsel, published a small notice in the local paper, formally stating his intentions (*Raleigh News and Observer*, July 11, 1935). Observing the appropriate forms and conventions, respondents were instructed to address their concerns to the parole board for deliberation and action, a process that would take several months.

NOTICE OF APPLICATION FOR PARDON

This is to give notice that the undersigned J.C. Walker will apply to His Excellency, the governor of North Carolina, for a pardon for the offense of murder in the second degree, said offense having been committed in the County of Brunswick, for which the undersigned is now serving a term of thirty years. All persons desiring to protest said application are notified to do so to commissioner of paroles immediately.

On this 10th day of July 1935.
J.C. Walker

And so things stood for a while.

13

ANOTHER TWIST OF THE TALE

SLAYER'S LONG VACATION ENDS

Walker Back in Cell After 22-Year Respite

North Carolina Paroles Man to Oklahoma Prison

Jesse C. Walker, Who Clemency in North Carolina, Returns to State.

OUT AGAIN; IN AGAIN

Paroled In Carolina Modern Jean Valjean Wanted In Oklahoma

NEW CHAPTER IN MANNING'S LIFE REVEALED

Oklahoma Files Detainer For Man Who Lived in Gulfport Before Admitting Old Time in Carolina

Manning Tells of Surrender

Wife in Gulfport Gets Letter Definitely Identifying Man at Raleigh, N. C.

'Conscience Convict' Faces Return to State Prison

Double Killer Who Surrendered After Reformation Is on Way to Oklahoma to Pay Another 'Debt'

RALEIGH, N. C. July 21—(P)— A 53-year-old escaped murderer who returned voluntarily to the penitentiary here after 16 years and became a jeweler. He married and was a respected member of his community. But his conscience pricked. He walked into Central

Walker bided his time at North Carolina's Central State Prison, from all accounts living up to his pledge to be a reformed man. He obediently followed the rules, participated in work assignments and generally behaved well. He may have used some of his time to polish his evangelism techniques. While petitions and

The *Biloxi Daily Record, Oklahoma City Daily Oklahoman, Chichasha Daily Express, Ardmore Daily Ardmorite* and *Miami Daily News Record*.

appeals from Mississippi were being collected, the authorities determined to keep Walker in custody for a year to validate his intentions and establish a record of exemplary behavior.

According to the Stanland family's memories, the son who had triggered Walker's earlier flight from Shallotte decided to actually pay him a visit in prison. Perhaps he wanted to make sure that he was indeed securely in custody. Sometime during their visit, Walker extended a hand through the bars as a gesture of friendship—or at least an appeal to sympathy—but was refused by his visitor, who could not bring himself to shake the hand of his father's murderer.

About ten months into Walker's stay at the prison, a letter was received by Warden H.H. Honeycutt from Warden Roy W. Kenny of the penitentiary in McAlester, Oklahoma. He asked for a detainer against Walker until it could be verified that he was the one who had killed a constable during a botched train robbery in 1909 and escaped from that state in 1914. (Remember Paul Williams?)

Once this news reached the papers, the letter resurrected narratives from twenty years earlier. It may be recalled that, at the time of Walker's apprehension in 1915, word surfaced that Walker was the Paul Williams who had fled Oklahoma the year before. Now, the newspapers were filled with recitations of the earlier offenses, at times with small differences but certainly getting the major points right. Walker was once again in the spotlight.

In Southport, the weekly newspaper, *The State Port Pilot*, had just started publishing under editor James M. Harper, and the Walker story was the most sensational feature in its early editions. Besides recapping elements of Walker's past, it noted that he had become a bit of a minor boogeyman, something to frighten children with. ("You be back home before dark, Edna Mae, or Jesse Walker gonna get you!") Nevertheless, an editorial (July 1, 1936) concluded with a plea for clemency, given his record of righteous behavior for more than fifteen years.

> *To some, it may seem hardly fair to grant amnesty to a man with a record like Walker had until about 1920. Remarkable, though, is his ability to completely reform and to change over to the life of a good citizen. We join with many other citizens of this section in the hope that Oklahoma State Prison officials will be as lenient with Walker as have been the prison authorities of North Carolina.*

Warden Kenny in Oklahoma may have noted Walker's return by way of the recently formed Federal Bureau of Investigation. Upon Walker's reincarceration, North Carolina authorities sent his fingerprints to the FBI, and that agency issued them in a routine advisory around the country for possible matches in other states. Under a different bureaucratic name, the agency had, for many years, maintained a repository of fingerprints to help identify criminals, especially if their crimes took them across state lines.

Something clicked for Warden Kenny, and he checked the FBI's information against his own files, where he found an apparent match and sent the fingerprints of one Paul Williams, an escapee from years before, to Washington. Following an official verification match with the prints of Walker, Warden Kenny sent the request for a detainer to his counterpart in North Carolina.

Warden H.H. Honeycutt in North Carolina was in an excellent position to be knowledgeable about such procedures; he was the first director of the State Bureau of Identification at the prison. Here, he instituted uniform and reliable identification documents for all offenders entering the prison system. Fingerprints, personal data and photographs were all summarized on intake cards and maintained in searchable and indexed files.

In addition to fingerprints, photographs were exchanged between the two wardens to further validate that Walker was indeed the Paul Williams of the Oklahoma incident. Walker had not mentioned Oklahoma in recent interviews or to his wife at the time. He may have assumed that the Oklahoma connection was lost to memory, having been made twenty-five years previously. He later suggested that he wished to serve out his earlier sentence until he was up for parole and then quietly go out west to turn himself in there. As earlier news stories resurfaced, he was forced to acknowledge that he had a further debt to pay.

So, Walker quietly demonstrated he was a model prisoner for a year while a considerable body of petitions in support of parole had built up. He had to notice the changes since his first incarceration at the prison. Warden Honeycutt had instituted a wide range of reforms in accordance with current social expectations placed on the penal system. There were large improvements in prisoners' health and hygiene, programs had been established to develop work skills and prepare prisoners for a hoped-for return to society, there was a better segregation of classes of prisoners to prevent conflicts and there were improved buildings and grounds all around the system. The system itself had also grown considerably, with smaller

port, N. C., Wednesday, July 1st, 1936   PUBLISHED EVERY WEDNESDAY $1.50 PER YEAR

rt's Commencement On Friday Night Well Attended

Finals Of Annual Daily Vacation Bible School Held In Southport High School Auditorium Before Good Audience

BRINGS TO CLOSE SUCCESSFUL TERM

Certificates Denoting Perfect Attendance And Satisfactory Completion Of Work Awarded 57

The commencement exercises Friday night in the high school auditorium, bringing to a close the annual Daily Vacation Bible School, was well attended by parents and others interested in the work.

Certificates for perfect attendance and satisfactory completion of work were awarded to 57 pupils at the exercises Friday night.

Attendance figures were not quite up to those of last year. A total of 139 pupils were enrolled, including 73 Baptists, 41 Methodists, 16 Presbyterians and 9 Episcopalians. Average daily attendance was 102.

The Rev. T. H. Biles, principal of the school, spoke in terms of warmest praise for members of the faculty in appreciation for their co-operation during the course of training.

Parole Granted Killer Of Brunswick County Sheriff

Jesse C. Walker Released Thursday From State Penitentiary In Raleigh, But Must Return To Oklahoma Prison

ONCE WAS FAMOUS OUTLAW OF COUNTY

After Killing Sheriff Stanland, Walker Broke Out Of Jail And Was Not Brought to Trial For Sometime

Jesse C. Walker, who more than a quarter of a century ago shot and fatally wounded Sheriff Jackson Stanland as the latter attempted to arrest him on some minor charge, was granted a parole Thursday.

The parole, however, was delivered into the hands of Oklahoma prison authorities. He escaped from that state in 1914 while serving a 30-year sentence for manslaughter. It is understood that friends and relatives will make every possible effort to secure a parole for Walker from this unfinished sentence.

Walker's case attracted nation-wide interest a year ago last April when he came to Raleigh from Gulfport, Miss., walked into the office of the prison warden and announced that he had returned to complete the unexpired time of his 30-year sentence for the slaying of the Brunswick county sheriff. Records revealed that he had escaped in 1919 af-

the most sensational in the history serving only 4 years. The movement which resulted in his parole was begun soon after his surrender.

The Walker case was one of (Continued on Page 8.)

Improvements In Equipment Used In Fire Control

Five-Room Houses Being Built For Look-Out At Three Towers In County; Telephone Connections Almost Complete

TO USE CONDEMNED TRUCKS NEXT YEAR

Board Of Education Donated 4 Condemned School Busses Which Will Be Stripped Down And Equipped

County Fire Warden Dawson Jones was in Southport Monday and announced that 5-room cottages are being constructed at three of the look-out towers in this county for the keeper and his family.

He also stated that the telephone line to the new look-out tower at Maco has been completed, connecting every tower in the county.

Members of the county board of education have donated four condemned school buses for use in the forest fire control work. According to Warden Jones these trucks will be stripped down and necessary repairs will be made. Water tanks and other equipment will then be installed and a truck will be stationed at each of the four towers in the county before the dry spell next year. This will give towermen an opportunity to go directly to small fires and to put them out before they have an opportunity to spread.

ey Recorder Hears Numerous Cases

Early Harvest Season

Begins In Brunswick Charles Drew

The local newspaper in Southport from 1935 detailed the voluntary surrender of Walker and summarized his earlier episodes of notoriety. Photos provided the basis for creating the drawings shown elsewhere. *Courtesy of The State Port Pilot, Southport, NC.*

regional facilities supplementing the crowded central prison. Even small improvements were not overlooked; the disciplinary whipping post was long gone, and mattresses were no longer filled with straw.

As Walker's case became more widely known, he began to be characterized as a modern-day "Jean Valjean," alluding to the Victor Hugo protagonist who escaped imprisonment and dedicated himself to a life of virtue. Granted, the analogy was a bit of stretch—killing two lawmen is not the same as stealing a loaf of bread, Walker had no Inspector Javert who relentlessly pursued him around the country and stolen pistols are nothing like silver candlesticks—but it was a handy device for headlines in the newspapers. It probably also helped that the very popular and Oscar-worthy *Les Misérables* was currently playing in theaters around the country, starring Fredric March and Charles Laughton.

After more back-and-forth discussion between authorities in the two states, it was decided that, should Walker be paroled in North Carolina, he would be surrendered directly to the Oklahoma authorities. As long as the Oklahoma authorities were assured of his delivery, they could patiently wait until the regular reviews and recommendations were complete before taking him into custody. However, despite Walker's apparent conversion to a life of good behavior, no one was taking any chances with trusting his word that he would actually act on his own volition to go back to Oklahoma.

In June 1936, Walker's case for parole came up for review. The petitions for clemency from his Mississippi friends had put him in good stead. In addition, some support was also received from parties in Columbus County, North Carolina, likely drummed up by kinfolk. Even the judge and prosecutor in in his 1915 murder trial came out in support of clemency. In approving the decision for parole, North Carolina governor J.C.B. Ehringhaus noted that Walker "lived the life of a good and useful citizen.…From a careful investigation, I have good reason to believe that the prisoner has reformed" (*Burlington Daily Times-News*, June 26, 1936).

With his North Carolina parole secured, Walker was held in custody to await Oklahoma officials to take him back to that state. In one jailhouse interview, he was rather coy and evasive about how he managed his 1919 escape. His rather naïve reason for keeping that secret was that he didn't want to give anyone else ideas about how to do it. In another interview, he took an upbeat view of his prospects, as recounted in the *Raleigh News and Observer* (July 17, 1936). Drawing some parallels with the Apostle Paul, Walker said that he, too, had seen the light and was a changed man. Quoting scraps of Bible verses as they might have lodged in his memory, he believed himself to be square with the Lord in heaven and was on a mission to settle his affairs here on Earth:

> *I had religion once and lost it. I thought I had it when I was a boy and joined the church, but I didn't. But I got religion, then lost it, and when you have it and lose it, you know it belonged to you. It's like you have a dollar in your pocket and lose it. And when you lose it, you realize what you had. I guess I'd like to preach—or maybe teach the Bible, although I haven't got much education. That's what I'll do when I get out, and in the meantime, I'm helping the prisoners I know as much as I can.*

Additional interviews suggested that Walker had been living for many years in a state of perpetual wariness and under a cloud of unresolved guilt. Nowhere in the narratives, however, is there an expression of remorse. Having turned himself in, he said, was a source of great relief, as he sought forgiveness of his debt to society. This kind of outlook had apparently carried him from Gulfport to Raleigh in the first place, and he was peacefully determined to fulfill his self-appointed mission.

Another journey awaited.

14

GO WEST, YOUNG MAN

PART TWO

I n about a week, Walker embarked on another journey. This time, he was a regular passenger, albeit with the enforced companionship of Oklahoma law officers. The 1,100-mile automobile trip would have taken a few days; where they stopped for overnight stays is unknown. The schedule may have brought them to towns with rooms for rent, or perhaps they patronized a couple of those recent "motor hotels" that were springing up alongside the newly improved highways. Here, the officers could rent a freestanding cabin and keep Walker out of circulation and under observation.

A growing network of decent highways made the journey far easier than Walker's first trip west in 1909. Traveling through North Carolina and passing into Tennessee, they made their way to Memphis, where they crossed the Mississippi River on the great Harahan Bridge. Then they traveled across Arkansas and into Oklahoma, eventually arriving at McAlester. Walker may have spent the long stretches studying his Bible. In between reading sessions, there might have been a never-ending store of tales or testimony. For his escorts, it might have made for a very long trip indeed.

Once they got to the penitentiary, which, at the time, was administered by Warden Roy W. Kenny, Walker was booked into the general population. He was registered as prisoner No. 1429, his original number from 1910, to await disposition of his case. A newspaper photograph from the time shows him in his heavy denim shirt and broad-striped pants, each stenciled with his number. He appears thinner than he was in his earlier years, is wearing glasses and has a head of unkempt white hair.

Warden Jess Dunn of the Oklahoma State Penitentiary at McAlester when Walker was paroled late in 1936. He instituted a number of reforms during his tenure, including the popular Prison Rodeo in 1940. He was killed during a prison break in 1941. *Photo courtesy of Oklahoma Historical Society.*

Governor E.W. Marland of Oklahoma, who reviewed Walker's appeals for clemency in 1936 and granted his parole and release. *Photo courtesy of Oklahoma Historical Society.*

His wife followed close behind; she made arrangements to take the train across the country to McAlester. She may have booked the trip on Southern Railways from Raleigh to Memphis, Tennessee, then changed to the Chicago, Rock Island and Pacific train to Oklahoma City, thence to McAlester to stay near the penitentiary. Repeating her activities from Walker's stay in Raleigh, Frances sought out a job in town and became a housekeeper or caregiver for an elderly physician and his wife (*Biloxi Daily Herald*, December 19, 1936). Here, she could earn a bit of a livelihood while awaiting the outcome of the events affecting her husband.

After more than a year of good behavior in North Carolina before being paroled in that state, Walker continued his good record at the Oklahoma Penitentiary. Petitions from friends and acquaintances in Gulfport served him well there, too. There were also the opinions of North Carolina authorities, who considered him wholly rehabilitated. Even W.J. Crump, the former prosecutor from Walker's Oklahoma trial in 1909, when he was known as Paul Williams, indicated that he would support a decision for parole if Walker's apparent reformation was determined to be genuine.

It may have been that Walker made good on his religious ambitions, too. He may have become something of a jailhouse evangelist among his fellow inmates, practicing on a literally captive audience in anticipation of a broader appeal outside. "If I should be paroled from Oklahoma," he said, "well, I reckon I'd become a roadside preacher. I might be able to keep a few wild fellows from doing the things I did" (*Raleigh News and Observer*, July 23, 1936). His theology may have been a bit sketchy, but he was earnest in maintaining his born-again outlook on life.

His case for clemency may have been supported by testimonials and his good behavior, but the wheels of bureaucracy move at their own speed, dictated by policies and procedures for such matters. It took some time for reports and forms to be completed and reviewed by the appropriate parties. As parts of the appeal fell into place, Walker's case was presented in accordance with the schedules for such deliberations.

Walker was paroled by Oklahoma governor E.W. Marland on November 24, 1936, just five months after receiving his North Carolina parole. He received his "walking papers" in anticipation of a return to Mississippi. Apparently, this was to be an unsupervised parole, granted under promises of good behavior and no further infractions. In the next couple of weeks, Walker was processed out of confinement and probably glad to leave his prison clothes behind. After reuniting with his wife, they made arrangements to travel the five hundred miles or so back to Gulfport, Mississippi, and the comfort of familiar surroundings.

Walker's traveling days were just about over.

15

IN THE MAGNOLIA STATE

PART TWO

fter his release in December 1936, Jesse went back with Frances to Gulfport, where they immediately sought out the county clerk's office and obtained a marriage license. They were remarried by Justice of the Peace Nat Bolton on December 10, this time with his correct name of Jesse C. Walker. A newspaper photograph of the pair shows Jesse in a suit and tie and Frances in a plain dark dress and light jacket. Neither of them appears to be comfortable with posing for the camera, and it is easily supposed that neither of them wanted the extra attention. Jesse may have still felt the burden of his past misdeeds, even while being glad to be out of prison. He hoped to eventually receive a full pardon and was resolved to live a righteous life in pursuit of that goal.

As reported in the *Biloxi Daily Herald* (December 19, 1936), the two of them returned to their home in what was described as a suburban location just east of Gulfport on Gulf Street. Despite the efforts of their neighbors, their house had been somewhat neglected during their year-and-a-half absence. They set about tidying up the place and settling claims for back property taxes. Among the pine trees, they reestablished a garden and even welcomed back a pet cat that had apparently been cared for by neighbors. For a while, the couple may have been aided by the largesse of friends and acquaintances who were glad to have them back in town.

The legal system was virtually done with Walker, and he was confident about his status with the Lord. However, Mother Nature may still have had something to say in the matter. In March 1937, just three months after the

When Jesse and Frances returned to Gulfport, Mississippi, following his parole in Oklahoma in 1936, they immediately sought a new marriage under their correct names, here recorded. *Public record, Department of Health, State of Mississippi.*

Walkers returned home, the *Biloxi Daily Herald* reported freakish lightning activity in the area. One of the reported incidents had lightning striking the metal fence around the Walkers' yard and welding the gate shut. Whatever symbolic significance that might have is best left to the imagination of the reader—just another odd tidbit from reports about his life.

In the 1940 United States census, Jesse and Frances Walker were both enumerated in Gulfport. His occupation was listed as "self-employed carpenter," although he had no wages at all in 1939 and was recorded as having more than forty weeks of unemployment at the time of the census. There was an indication that he had income from other sources; perhaps he had gone back on the relief rolls. If so, the relief payments would have been very modest, so the couple lived accordingly and kept expenses low. It is not known if Jesse ever fulfilled his mission of becoming a "sidewalk soul-saver." It is more likely that he gradually abandoned that idea, although he continued to be an active member of a church congregation.

Walker had never established an occupation or solid trade, and he evidently felt no need to advance his education beyond the fifth grade. It might be that he found a few unskilled jobs just before the country entered World War II and labor needs had to be filled by those who were not called into the military. Gulfport obtained land for a new airport in 1941, and the army launched ambitious projects for bomber training and facilities to house servicemen. In addition, Keesler Air Base was being constructed just a few miles to the east in Biloxi. Then, too, boatbuilding increased dramatically in shipyards all along the Mississippi coast. The population of the area grew dramatically, driven by military activity, construction trades and commercial enterprises.

In 1940, Frances was evidently the main breadwinner, working busily as a home-based seamstress throughout the previous year, perhaps on a piecework basis. Her wages were unexceptional, coming to an average of some fifty-five dollars a month. She may have continued this work as the population swelled in the coastal communities; off-the-rack garments were still a long way from replacing made-from-scratch clothes. Habits from the Depression years still favored making do, and clothes would always need altering, mending or refitting.

In 1944, word came from Oklahoma that Walker's petition for pardon had at last been processed and that it was approved by Governor Robert S. Kerr. Finally dispensing of this last bit of pending business, Walker could feel that he was square with the law. Whatever conscience-easing changes he had adopted since his enlightenment in the 1930s, it still would have been a relief to be free of the lingering burdens of his previous life. At last, he could feel that he was "shed of his time," as he said when he turned himself in at the Central State Prison in North Carolina in 1935.

Around this time, a late photograph shows Walker in a much different presentation. About sixty years old, he looks somewhat haggard and drawn, lacking the roundness of his face that characterized his earlier appearance. His hair, certainly still white, now had more of a wiry look to it and his eyes

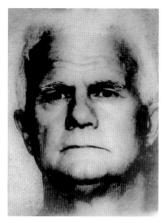

Opposite: Jesse Walker's death certificate from the State of Mississippi. Indications are that he died from stomach cancer, which was likely a condition he had endured for a number of years. *Public record, Department of Health, State of Mississippi.*

Left: Later in life, Walker sent a photo and a brief apology note to his first wife, Rosa Lee, who by that time had remarried (and was widowed) and was living in Rocky Mount, North Carolina. It was retrieved from Rosa Lee's personal effects after she died in 1962. *Photo courtesy of J.R. Robinson, Robinson family history.*

Below: The double gravestone for Jesse and Frances in Evergreen Cemetery in Gulfport, Mississippi. *From Find-A-Grave, www.findagrave.com.*

had receded a bit and darkened from their earlier light blue. Overall, there is a look of pained intensity, as if he was experiencing some kind of long-term discomfort. Whatever expression he had of calm purpose in earlier photographs seemed to be diminished.

In an unwelcome turn of events, his cast-off burdens were now replaced with a diagnosis of cancer of the stomach in 1945. He may have felt the symptoms of that condition for some years before the diagnosis. Progress of the growth prevented any surgical remedy—the only approach that would have been available at the time—and he went into a prolonged decline. The tumorous growth spread over the next ten months, and after four days in a terminal phase, Walker died on July 26, 1946.

Following a service at a local funeral home, Walker was buried in Evergreen Cemetery in Gulfport. In a bit of foresight, a double plot had been purchased so that Frances could someday be laid to rest next to her husband. Frances was twenty years younger than Jesse, however, and still had a lot of living to do. She remarried, became Frances Vincent and survived Jesse by nearly forty years, passing away in 1985.

AFTERWORD

After all of this, one desires to find some kind of connective thread woven through all the episodes and exploits of Jesse Walker (also known as Paul Williams and Frank C. Manning). There are plenty of gaps in his story that one can be curious about. How did he subsist during his travels between North Carolina and Oklahoma and back again? What rationale led him to stick around in rural Mississippi and get married a second time? Where did he pick up the skills to pass himself off as a jeweler or watch and clock repairer? How did he and Frances manage to live between 1920 and 1926, when they ended up in Gulfport?

Walker would probably have been glad to fill in the gaps had he been asked. From bits of published comments, he certainly was not a reluctant interview subject. His habit, though, was to embroider his accounts with exaggerations and outright fabrications, but they were related in such a way to be at least marginally credible. He certainly was not reluctant to engage others in conversation, and with enough sincerity, such tales would tend to be accepted. About 80 percent of his life was spent below the radar; it is tempting to speculate on his other adventures.

I don't think this narrative is an apologist kind of work. Walker did not seem to be an unlikeable fellow. Out in the open, he was friendly and confident—perhaps a bit too much so. He was also an easy conversationalist once you understood that he tended to be loose with the accuracy of his comments. Other than one sensational incident, there is no indication that he was a problem drinker—or that he was a drinker at all. Likewise, his story

The map shows Walker's locations over the course of his life, based on reports of newspapers that covered various incidents related to him. At least until 1920, it is likely he hopped trains for most of his travel; a growing network of decent highways after that time provided him more opportunities to hitchhike. *Map by author, 2022.*

gives no hints that he was a gambler or a libertine or an abusive person. His marriages seem have been marked by affection and constancy, despite distractions along the way.

Walker obviously had issues with confinement. He chafed under regulatory or physical restrictions, whether they were imposed by schooling, military regimentation, employment or penal discipline of various kinds. His discomfort may have stemmed from a deep-seated attitude of personal freedom established in his youth. That was where he spent at least ten formative years in an unstructured lifestyle, largely away from established society and societal expectations. Such a foundation may have permanently affected his outlook on life, where rules and their enforcement seemed to be unfairly placed on him.

He may have harbored biases and prejudices common for the times and his formative years, but he was not outspoken about them. And there is no evidence that he ever held political beliefs; it is easily supposed that he never voted at all. His narrative also suggests that he was comfortable with unemployment. Evidence of any enduring livelihood is scarce; most of his time seems to have been spent in an itinerant trade or self-employed.

That being said, he certainly did some unlikeable things. They do not seem to have been very carefully thought out, and his impulses took over when limits were imposed on his freedom to act. Obviously, he was not one to take kindly to confinement and was aggressive when cornered, certainly so with a weapon in his hand. His petty thefts and the store-breaking incidents were perhaps more crimes of opportunity than indicators of a pattern of intent. And he clearly did not plan to embark on a career of infamy—nor did he plan anything at all. Other than a few sensational events concentrated in a ten-year arc of notoriety, there wasn't a trail of misdeeds to follow through the years.

Whatever divine benefit he received after his conversion in the 1930s is beyond the purview of this book. He tried to study scripture and glean insights where he could, latching on to a few applicable Bible verses and perhaps knitting them together in imaginative ways. If one accepts his story of a quest for atonement at face value, it suggests that he was heeding some form of conscience. In the end, he seems to have come to terms with the deeds of a turbulent decade in his life and was resolved to settle down. Nothing after his final discharge from Oklahoma suggests the pattern of drifting and grifting that determined so much of the course of his earlier years.

There is a final item of curiosity, although it is highly speculative. In 1932, it was noted that Walker was apparently enlightened after attending revival services. In that same year, Warner Brothers released the popular feature film *I Am a Fugitive from a Chain Gang*, starring Paul Muni and directed by Mervyn LeRoy. It is a gritty, dark drama with a strong appeal for penal reform, but it portrays some striking parallels to Walker's own experiences—unfair arrest, two prison escapes, establishing a repurposed life, voluntary surrender, hope for a parole and more. It was a highly praised movie based on a true story serialized in the popular *True Detective* magazine the year before. Perhaps Walker read the story or managed to see the movie in Biloxi or Gulfport and identified with certain elements of the plot. He might have even found some inspiration for his later efforts of reconciliation in 1935. Or maybe it is just another of those odd coincidences he had in life.

Anecdotes from the Robinson family's history helped shed light on various aspects of Walker's relationship with the Leonard family, his friendship with young Frank Leonard, his courtship of Rosa Lee Leonard, the death of his

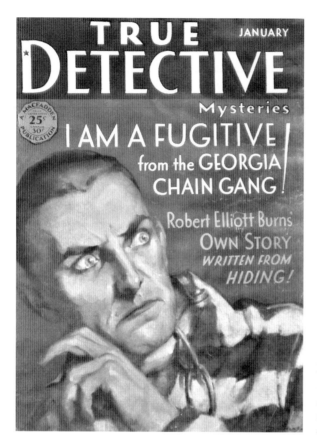

The cover of the popular *True Detective* magazine from January 1931. The featured story contained the account of an escaped convict with parallels to Walker's own experiences; the next year, it was turned into a highly regarded movie starring Paul Muni. *Author's collection.*

daughter Clara Lee Walker and more. In later years, if Walker was discussed at all—and never with children present—it was done in hushed tones as the grown-ups gathered for after-meal conversation at family gatherings. Bits and pieces of the story achieved a certain durability, although with tellings and retellings, remembrances softened some of the details. Far fonder recollections were held for Rosa Lee, who maintained a lively personality throughout her life.

TIMELINE FOR JESSE C. WALKER

1882 or 1883: Born in Columbus County, North Carolina (maybe Bulloch County, Georgia).

1889–94: Schooled in Columbus County, North Carolina.

1898: Leaves Columbus County and travels to Georgia (perhaps to immediate family).

1902–3: Sells organs in Claxton, Georgia, is suspected of embezzlement and flees area.

1903: Moves back to Columbus County, North Carolina.

1905: Marries Rosa Lee Leonard near Shallotte in Brunswick County, North Carolina.

1906: Returns to Georgia with his wife, displays disruptive behavior and returns alone to North Carolina.

1907: His wife returns to Brunswick County with their daughter (who was born in Georgia).

1907: Joins and deserts the army.

1908: Kills Brunswick County sheriff in Shallotte and breaks out of jail in 1909.

1909: Kills law officer in Oklahoma (as Paul Williams).

1910–14: Incarcerated at Oklahoma State Prison (escapes).

1915: Returns to North Carolina and is then spotted and captured in Wilmington.

1915–19: Incarcerated at North Carolina Central Prison (escapes).

1920: Marries Frances Britt in Crawford, Mississippi (as Frank Manning).

1920–26: Lives in West Point, Meridian and Houston, Mississippi.

1926: Moves to Gulfport, Mississippi, where he is involved in door-to-door jewelry sales and watch repair.

1932: Experiences conversion and desires to make up for his wrongdoings.

1935: Returns to Raleigh, North Carolina, to turn himself in at Central Prison.

1936: Paroled in North Carolina and returns to Oklahoma, where he is also paroled. He then remarries in Gulfport, Mississippi.

1940: Listed in U.S. census in Gulfport, Mississippi.

1944: Pardoned in Oklahoma.

1946: Jesse Walker dies (age sixty-three).

1962: Rosa Lee (his first wife) dies (age seventy-five).

1985: Frances Walker (as Frances Vincent) dies (age eighty-one).

DENOUEMENTS

Photograph courtesy of J.R. Robinson.

Rosa Lee: For much of this, I am indebted to the Robinson family history, as compiled by J.R. Robinson. His grandmother was Rosa Lee's sister, and she married Charles B. Robinson, the brother of one of the officers who witnessed Sheriff Stanland's shooting and later became Brunswick County sheriff in his own right. This connection and the extensive intermarriage of families in lower Brunswick County led to a preservation of oral accounts that were valuable.

For quite a few years, the last Rosa Lee Walker would have known of her husband's whereabouts was in 1919, the year of his escape from the North Carolina Central Prison. Jesse was long gone, nobody knew where, and no word had been received from him for year after year. In 1923, she moved to Rocky Mount, North Carolina, with a couple of relations. Sometime during this period, she obtained a divorce on grounds of abandonment, although the decree document remains elusive. In 1928, she married Ben Edwards, a widower ten years her senior, in Rocky Mount. The marriage license includes her maiden name, Leonard, handwritten among the other typewritten entries on the form. Edwards died in 1935, and Rosa Lee decided to remain in Rocky Mount and lived in the same house from then on, along with her sister and brother. In the early 1950s, she was diagnosed with breast cancer and underwent a double mastectomy, which arrested the condition for a while. The cancer returned, however, and in 1962, she died and was buried in Rocky Mount next to the grave of her brother.

Frances: After Walker's death in 1946, Frances apparently remained in Gulfport. She acted as Walker's executrix in duly publishing legal notices for creditors against his modest estate and took care of settling his other affairs. We do not know what kind of conversations they had during or after Walker's times in the penitentiaries in North Carolina and Oklahoma, but Frances persevered and stood by him during those trying months. Even after their remarriage in 1936 and for the next ten years, she persisted in calling him "Frank," the name by which she first made his acquaintance in 1920, during his Mississippi stay. The couple had no children. Frances probably stayed active in church activities, and at some point, she married again. She survived Walker by nearly forty years, dying in 1985. She was buried with the name Frances Vincent next to Walker in Evergreen Cemetery in Gulfport.

Minnie: Minnie Stanland was overwhelmed with grief when her husband was killed in 1908. She was twenty-nine years old, and they had been married for only twelve years. She spent most of that time pregnant, enduring the toll of that condition, having borne nine children. Seven of these children survived infancy, and in 1908, they ranged in age from eleven years old to nine months old. A hoped-for larger house was now out of the question. Stanland's business partners took over his property and commercial affairs; they were reportedly stingy in supporting Minnie and the children. She probably

Photograph courtesy of Clinton Stanland.

got some support from family, but she declined and died in 1912 at the age of thirty-one and was buried next to her husband in Shallotte. The children, now bereft of parents, were taken in by the late sheriff's business partners, who also assumed possession of his properties, businesses and financial resources. Family memories say that the children saw very little benefit or support from their guardians, and they were much embittered by their situation. They grew up and moved on but retained enough of their painful memories to oppose Walker's plea for clemency in 1935.

Appendix C

ASSOCIATED NAMES

J esse Walker's "career" spanned several decades and was touched by many individuals in various walks of life and in many locations. Significant mentions in published accounts (a call of authorial discretion) are listed here in close chronological order, along with the first year of mention, where applicable. Walker's aliases have been removed for clarity.

Rosa Lee Leonard: sister of Frank A., married Walker in 1905, remarried under her maiden name in 1928

Clara Lee Walker: daughter of Jesse and Rosa Lee Walker (1907–1918), died of pneumonia/influenza

Frank M. Leonard: local farmer, merchant, Walker's father-in-law (1908)

Frank A. Leonard: youthful confederate of Walker in Shallotte (1908), son of a prominent local family

C.D. Robinson: justice of the peace who officiated Walker's wedding at the house of Ben Robinson in Lockwood's Folly (1905) with witnesses C.O. Robinson, Alfred Robinson and R.R. Robinson

Jackson Stanland (1862–1908): shot in 1908 by Walker; Minnie (née Hewett, wife, died in 1911), Herman (son), Thomas (son), Chancey (son), Edward (son), Bessie (daughter), Catherine (daughter) and Murphy (son) were petitioners opposing clemency for Walker in 1935

J.E. Robinson, A.S. White and James Long: Brunswick County sheriff deputies who accompanied Sheriff Jackson Stanland to serve a warrant on Walker (1908)

J. Arthur Dosher, J.A. Stone, ——— Goley: physicians present at Jackson Stanland's death (1908)

James Williams: owned the home where Jackson Stanland died after being shot (1908)

J.J. Knox: of El Paso, succeeded Jackson Stanland as Brunswick County sheriff, directed immediate local response and manhunt through the Green Swamp after Walker's escape from Southport (1908)

Warren Mintz: guard on duty at Southport Jail just before Walker's escape (1909)

J.B. Fountain: Southport jailer injured in Walker's escape (1909)

William Dudley: young accomplice of Walker who joined him in escaping Southport Jail (1908)

D.G. Hewett: Jackson Stanland's business partner in Shallotte and Lockwood's Folly (1909)

W.W. Kitchin: North Carolina governor, authorized reward for Walker after Southport escape (1909)

J.W. Brooks: of Wilmington, local businessman who helped coordinate communications with authorities after Walker's apprehension and escape (1909)

D.R. Johnson, J.H. Thompson, R.S. Pinner, ——— Applewhite, C.O. Knox, ——— Mincey, ——— Edmundson and William E. Maultsby: named members of various posses and search parties in the manhunt for Walker after his escape from Southport (1909)

George Johnson Kirk: Brewer Township deputy constable killed in gunfight following a foiled train robbery near Braggs, Oklahoma (1909)

——— Wicks: Brewer Township constable wounded in a gunfight following a foiled train robbery near Braggs, Oklahoma (1909)

Fred McDonald and Fred Wright: accomplices in foiled Oklahoma train robbery, captured in Proctor (1909)

——— **Ramsey,** ——— **Brucker and** ——— **Hamilin:** sheriff and deputies in Oklahoma who led search for two fugitives from foiled train robbery (1909)

W.J. Crump: Muskogee County prosecutor in the 1909 Oklahoma train robbery and killing, advocate for Walker's parole (1936)

Irvin B. Tucker: Whiteville attorney, contacted by Walker prior to his capture in Wilmington (1915)

J.W. Dixon: of Supply, North Carolina, master of small schooner, recognized Walker in Wilmington and alerted authorities (1915)

George Harriss: Wilmington justice of the peace, issues arrest warrant for Walker (1915)

A.L. Kelly, John Davis, H. Mack Godwin, D.W. Coleman, Leon George and Charles H. Jones: Wilmington posse that apprehended Walker when he returned (1915)

S.P. Cowan: sheriff of New Hanover County, took custody of Walker, contact with Oklahoma authorities (1915)

J.E. Robinson: Brunswick County sheriff, previously a deputy present at the 1908 shooting of Jackson Stanland, took custody of Walker from Wilmington after his reappearance there (1915)

——— **Russ:** Southport jailer at the time of Walker's return (1915)

R.W. Davis: Southport attorney, prosecutor of Walker (1915), helped negotiate North Carolina parole (1936)

William J. Bellamy: Wilmington attorney retained to represent Walker (1915)

M.H. Justice: judge for Brunswick County Superior Court, presided over Walker's arraignment and request for change of venue (1915)

Robert W. Dick: warden of Oklahoma penitentiary, led to Walker being identified as Paul Williams (1915)

J.J. Johnson: physician from Oklahoma who treated Walker's immediate wounds (1909), identified Walker when he returned (1915)

——— **Cranmer, R.W. Davis, H.L. Lyon and C.E. McCullen:** prosecuting team in the Pender County trial after Walker's return (1915)

George Rountree: judge who presided at Pender County trial for Walker (1915), later supported clemency at North Carolina parole hearing (1936)

James Collie: superintendent at North Carolina Central Prison when Walker escaped (1919)

Frances (née Britt) Manning/Walker: married Jesse Walker as Frank Manning (1920 in Crawford, Mississippi), then remarried him under his correct name in 1936

H.H. Honeycutt: warden at North Carolina Central Prison (1935)

M.S. Conner: governor of Mississippi (1932–36) to whom clemency petitions were sent for forwarding to North Carolina after Walker turned himself in (1935)

J.C.B. Ehringhaus: governor of North Carolina (1933–37), to whom petitions for and against clemency were addressed, paroled Walker (1935)

Edwin M. Gill: parole commissioner in North Carolina (1935)

Roy W. Kenny: warden at Oklahoma State Prison (1936)

Homer L. Lyon: state solicitor at Walker's parole hearing in 1936, had previous experience with Walker's 1915 return (1936)

Irvin B. Tucker: parole counsel for Walker (1936)

E.W. Marland: governor of Oklahoma at the time of Walker's parole and return to Mississippi (1936)

Nat Bolton: justice of the peace in Gulfport, Mississippi, who remarried Jesse and Frances as Walker (1936)

Robert S. Kerr: governor of Oklahoma who signed off on Walker's decree of pardon (1944)

BIBLIOGRAPHY

Anderson, Nels. *The Hobo: The Sociology of the Homeless Man.* Chicago: University of Chicago Press, 1923.
(This book is unrelated to the narrative of Walker's life, but it is the first significant study of the mobile class of individuals known as "hobos." About half of the book details the character and nature of hobo origins, lifestyle and behavior, as derived from extensive participant/observer experiences with the population under study.)

Brunswick County Recorder of Deeds, public records.

Census of the United States, 1900, 1910, 1920 and 1940.

City Directory. Gulfport, MS: 1931, 146.

Cosgriff, Chris. "Officer Down Memorial Page." www.odmp.org. (Information on fallen law enforcement officers.)

Family Search. "Georgia, County Marriages, 1785-1950." www.familysearch.org. (Database with images.)

Harrison County, Mississippi, public records.

Hinkle, William G., and Gregory S. Taylor. *North Carolina State Prison.* Charleston, SC: Arcadia Publishing, 2016.

Koenig, Mark W. *The Wilmington, Brunswick & Southern Railroad.* Charleston, SC: Arcadia Publishing, 2022.

North Carolina Newspaper Collection, State Archives of North Carolina.

Public Documents of the State of North Carolina. "Biennial Reports of the State Prison Department (1920s and 1930s)." Raleigh, NC: North Carolina Digital Collection, North Carolina State Publication. (Although most of these make for pretty dry reading, the report of 1930–32 offers a very good overview of beneficial changes and reforms instituted during the previous ten years.)

———. "Prison Superintendent's Report (1913)." Raleigh, NC: North Carolina Digital Collections.

Serafino, Jason. "Leon Ray Livingston, America's Most Famous Hobo." www.mentalfloss.com.

State Archives of North Carolina. "Minutes of the Superior Court 1807–1966." Pender County, June 1915.

State Library of North Carolina, North Carolina Department of Natural and Cultural Resources. NCpedia. www.ncpedia.org. (Online collection of contributed verified articles about many aspects of North Carolina's history and culture.)

Vernon, Tom. "The Story of Sheriff Jackson Stanland & Deputy Isaac William Skipper." *North Carolina Peace Officer* 26, no. 1 (Summer 1997): 10–16.

Wilmington, N.C. Directory, 1913–1914. Richmond, VA: Hill Directory Company, 1913–14.

Newspapers

The online digital compilations of *newspapers.com*, *newspaperarchive.com*, *gateway.okhistory.org* and *digitalnc.org* provided access to many publications, and searches for relevant terms yielded results from these publications. With a network of telegraphic dispatches, identical stories could be found in quite a few newspapers, occasionally attributed to a source publication.

Charlotte News (Charlotte, NC)
Citizen-Times (Asheville, NC)
Daily Ardmoreite (Ardmore, OK)
Daily Chieftain (Vinita, OK)
Daily Eagle (Bryan, TX)
Daily Eagle (Enid, OK)
Daily Express (Chickasha, OK)
Daily Herald (Biloxi, MS)
Daily Herald (Delphos, OH)
Daily Herald (Shawnee, OK)
Daily Leader (Guthrie, OK)
Daily Light (Waxahachie, TX)

Daily News (Galveston, TX)
Daily News (Greensboro, NC)
Daily News-Record (Miami, OK)
Daily Oklahoman (Oklahoma City, OK)
Daily Record (Hickory, NC)
Daily Times-News (Burlington, NC)
Daily Tribune (Concord, NC)
Eastern Reflector (Greenville, NC)
Evening Chronicle (Charlotte, NC)
Evening News (Ada, OK)
Evening Times (Raleigh, NC)
Greensboro Patriot (Greensboro, NC)

Leader Call (Laurel, MS)

Lincoln Times (Lincolnton, NC)

Morning Examiner (Bartlesville, OK)

Morning Star (Wilmington, NC)

Moulton Eagle (Moulton, TX)

New Bern Weekly Journal (New Bern, NC)

News & Observer (Raleigh, NC)

New-State Tribune (Muskogee, OK)

North Carolinian (Raleigh, NC)

Oklahoma State Capital (Guthrie, OK)

Review (High Point, NC)

Robesonian (Lumberton, NC)

Sapulpa Herald (Sapulpa, OK)

Sapulpa Light (Sapulpa, OK)

Semi-Weekly Messenger (Wilmington, NC)

Smithfield Herald (Smithfield, NC)

State Port Pilot (Southport, NC)

Sun Herald (Biloxi, MS)

Talala Gazette (Talala, OK)

Times Democrat (Muskogee, OK)

Weekly Observer (Fayetteville, NC)

Western Sentinel (Winston-Salem, NC)

Wilmington Dispatch (Wilmington, NC)

Interviews

The author interviewed Rich Sullivan (Southport Jail), J.R. Robinson (Leonard family connection to Walker), Clinton Stanland (descendant of Jackson Stanland) and staff at Jim's Pawn and Guns Shop in Wilmington, North Carolina (information on old handguns, along with their features and actions).

Drawings

Mitchell Henderson (His Lead Studio)

ABOUT THE AUTHOR

Mark Koenig was born and raised in Milwaukee, Wisconsin. After earning bachelor's and master's degrees in business, he worked for eighteen years in healthcare management, particularly in the areas of planning and strategic development. These activities provided the understanding that events are rarely linear. Instead, they require a framework that organizes, connects and relates many factors that influence the flow of events.

After a move to Wilmington, North Carolina, he had the opportunity to direct the Wilmington Railroad Museum, just in time to launch a new era in interpreting and presenting the story of railroad history and heritage. All the exhibits needed to be recomposed and reinterpreted, a project that required research into and analysis of the many interwoven facets of railroad growth and development. This would prove to be an ongoing effort, as new information came to light and had to be incorporated into the narratives at the museum.

It was here where the seeds of Koenig's first book were found, where the story of a local short-line railroad could be examined in depth, weaving together history, old recollections, geography, economic forces and insights about personalities. Spinning out from that narrative were the threads for this second book about Jesse C. Walker, which explores at length a character mentioned in an episode in the earlier work. Once again, the story integrates a narrative of news accounts, geography, insights about personalities and family information.

Koenig and his wife live in Leland, North Carolina.